ANCIENT ITALY

COVER

Bronze figure of Turms (the Etruscan Hermes). Found at Uffington, Oxfordshire, Mrs A. E. Preston bequest, H. 0.22 [1943.38]. 5th century BC.

UNIVERSITY OF OXFORD
ASHMOLEAN MUSEUM

ANCIENT ITALY BEFORE THE ROMANS

By

A . C . B R O W N

with a bibliography by
D. R I D G W A Y

ASHMOLEAN MUSEUM OXFORD

1980

ASHMOLEAN MUSEUM PUBLICATIONS
Archaeology, History & Classical Studies

Treasures of the Ashmolean
Ancient Cyprus
Ancient Egypt
Ancient Iran
Ancient Iraq
Archaeology, Artefacts and the Bible
The Arundel Vases
Greek Vases
Scythian Treasures in Oxford

Set in Times Roman and printed in Great Britain by
Cheney and Sons Ltd., Banbury, Oxfordshire.

Acknowledgements

Mr Humphrey Case, Keeper of the Department of Antiquities, has kindly read the text of this booklet and I am most grateful to him and to Dr Roger Moorey, Acting Keeper during the time it was being written, for their help and encouragement. I am deeply indebted to Mr David Ridgway of Edinburgh University for reading and making many valuable suggestions on the draft and for preparing the extensive bibliography; to Professor John Boardman, Mr Michael Vickers and Dr. Andrew Sherratt for their helpful comments. Mrs Pat Clarke drew the maps and figures. Mrs Jane Barlow patiently typed the text and Miss O. Godwin prepared the photographs except for plate 1 (copyright Pitt Rivers Museum) and plate XVIII taken by Mr R. Wilkins.

Notes for the Reader

1. The booklet is designed as a brief guide to the Italic and Etruscan antiquities displayed in the John Evans Room in the Department of Antiquities. It is therefore necessarily biased towards the Ashmolean collection. The imported Greek vases found in Italy and the objects made in the Greek colonies of southern Italy and Sicily are exhibited in the Beazley Room and the Sunken Court and are not included here.

2. The numbers which appear in square brackets in the plate captions are the Museum accession numbers.

3. Measurements are given in parts of a metre. The following abbreviations are used. H. =height; L. =length; W. =width and D. =diameter.

4. The form most familiar to the English reader has been used for place-names.

v

Contents

I. Introduction

BRITISH INVOLVEMENT IN ITALIAN ARCHAEOLOGY

The study of ancient art and archaeology in Italy has a long history dating from the Renaissance. Interest was then centred primarily on Rome, where the most impressive remains of ancient buildings still stood. As early as the fifteenth century AD collections of 'antiques' were made in Florence as well as Rome, mainly by Italian prelates and merchants. Most of the objects were Roman, but already, thanks mainly to the fanciful theories of Annius of Viterbo (1432-1502), a web of 'mystery' was being spun round the Etruscans, the most important people in Italy before the Romans. A mystery which is perpetuated in popular writing to this day.

British involvement with ancient Italy and the Etruscans, apart from Thomas Dempster's *De Etruria Regali* written between 1616 and 1625, began in the eighteenth century when Dempster's book was eventually published. British aristocrats travelling in Italy were stimulated by discoveries at Herculaneum and Pompeii and by the dispersal of some local private collections. They formed societies and collections of their own to promote interest in ancient Italy. Of these societies that of the Dilettanti, which first met in 1732, was the most famous. One of its members was William Hamilton, Envoy Extraordinary to the Court of Naples from 1764, whose first collection, mainly of vases passed eventually to the British Museum. The collection had been published in four impressive volumes. Although these did not have a wide readership, they had a considerable influence on arbiters of taste, among them Sir Josiah Wedgwood. Already a successful potter, Wedgwood set up a new factory to specialise in 'ornamental' rather than 'useful' wares in 1769. This factory in Staffordshire he called Etruria. Six commemorative vases were produced to celebrate the opening. These were decorated with figures copied from a Greek vase, an Attic red figure hydria by the Meidias Painter found in Italy, illustrated by Hamilton and now in the British Museum. At this time such vases were generally believed to be Etruscan. Beneath the figures were the words 'Artes Etruriae Renascuntur'. For those who could not afford to travel and buy objects in Etruria, Italy, there was now the opportunity to obtain copies from Etruria, England. By the end of the eighteenth century travellers and scholars had turned their attention to Greece and Etruria was momentarily eclipsed.

The discovery at Vulci in Etruria in 1828 of a vast necropolis containing thousands of vases revived interest in Italian antiquities. Most of the decorated vases were imports from Greece. Already in the eighteenth century scholars had begun differentiating the various wares found in Italy, but the discoveries at Vulci only served to put the clock back in this respect, for many scholars did not believe that there could have been such a huge trade in vases from Greece to Italy. The chief landowner at Vulci was Lucien Bonaparte, Prince of Canino, who insisted that all vases discovered on his estates were made locally. As well as Vulci such famous Etruscan sites as Tarquinia, Chiusi and Orvieto were soon under investigation.

Etruscan antiquities were introduced to the British public by a memorable exhibition opened in January 1837 at 121 Pall Mall by the Campanari brothers of Toscanella (Tuscania)—whose excavating partnership with the Papal Government resulted, also in 1837, in the establishment of the Museo Etrusco Gregoriano in the Vatican. The Pall Mall exhibition was remarkable not only for its contents but also for the extraordinarily 'modern' attitude to the display itself. One visitor recalled that 'The judicious manner in which the rooms of the exhibition were fitted up, to represent the real sepulchral chambers, gave nearly as perfect a representation as could be obtained by a visit to the tombs themselves; the reality was, in a great measure, brought before the eyes of the spectators. Many of those antiquities are now in the British Museum, where, in their unarranged state, they are passed by with but little, if any, attention; . . . so much has arrangement to do with exciting public interest.' The impact of the Campanari exhibition on contemporary taste in London was considerable; and not the least significant effect for Italian archaeological studies in Britain was the conversion of Mrs Hamilton Gray, an indefatigable traveller but inaccurate authority, to 'Etruscology'. Her 500-page book, *Tour to the Sepulchres of Etruria in 1839*, was first published in 1840. In 1842, George Dennis, a 28-year old clerk in the Excise Office, made the first of several tours in Etruria: and in 1848 he published the first edition of his classic *Cities and Cemeteries of Etruria*, designed in part at least to 'supply the deficiencies' of Mrs Hamilton Gray's book as a practical guide for 'those swarms of our countrymen who annually traverse that classic region in their migrations between Florence and Rome'. One hundred years later, John Bradford—the Oxford pioneer of aerial photography in Italian archaeology—declared that 'In several instances, Dennis's descriptions of sites, compiled from his own field-work, still remain the best available' Dennis's Victorian masterpiece is, in fact, the best guide book to Etruria (whether read at home or on the spot), and it is still treated as the indispensable starting point for topographical investigation by all serious field-workers in this area.

The early excavations in Etruria were nearly all of cemeteries and were pure treasure hunts. Plain unpainted pottery was usually thrown away, or at best given to interested onlookers. One such excavation took place as late as 1892 near Chianciano, when a grave was opened as a diversion to entertain a Miss Eliza Thomas, who was taking the waters at Chiusi with her sister and Italian brother-in-law. She was allowed to choose from the plainer wares found in the tomb, 'So she chose what she thought was most

2

representative'. These vases were later given to the Ashmolean (Fig. 14, c, e-g). In Italy large and small collections were formed by private persons as well as museums. Collectors were often also dealers, working from their own homes or from shops. Visits to such people were well described by Mrs Hamilton Gray, who tells a story against herself which also illustrates the widespread influence of Wedgwood imitations. When visiting a priest's house she saw an object which: 'I conjectured . . . had been presented to him by some English traveller . . . it consisted of a small and well-finished tray . . . and this tray was filled with a variety of small cups and sugar-basins . . . I looked out of the window, praised two or three prints in the room, and then asked with a careless air what was the use of that china-stand upon the buffet. The good priest smiled, and said that it was a focalare which he had got out of a scavo a few weeks before! I forgot all my prudence and exclaimed 'So it really does come from a tomb and it is ancient! How extraordinary! I took it for a Wedgwood dejeuné' (cf. Fig. 14, g).

In 1829 the Instituto di Corrispondenza Archeologica was founded in Rome, largely at the instigation of E. Gerhard. He was one of a circle of scholars, known as the Roman Hyperboreans, who studied not only the antiquities of Rome and the surrounding areas, but also the lesser known antiquities in Naples, southern Italy and Sicily. Some objects reported in the early publications of the Instituto are now in the Ashmolean collection (see for example Pls. IX, XXX). Two generous benefactors of the Museum were members, Edmund Oldfield and Charles Drury Fortnum. By the end of the century it was thought that British scholarly interests would be well served by the establishment of a school modelled on the existing School at Athens. In 1901 the British School at Rome was opened welcoming not only scholars and students but also visitors 'desiring to pursue serious studies in Rome'. Many of those visiting the School brought back antiquities which they subsequently gave to the Ashmolean. In more recent years, the School has kept up the British tradition begun by George Dennis with an extensive programme of field survey in southern Etruria; and it has also been responsible, with the Rome University Istituto di Etruscologia, for the excavation and publication (*Notizie degli Scavi* 1963-1976) of a large Villanovan cemetery at Veii.

The greater part of the Ashmolean's collection of Italian antiquities was thus acquired during the last decades of the nineteenth and the early years of the twentieth centuries. Comparatively little comes from excavations, and most of the objects were acquired through dealers, either directly by the Museum or by benefactors. The Italian material in the Museum has to be re-assessed periodically in the light of new developments achieved by archaeologists working in Italy—where excavations, exhibitions and publications still combine to excite the interest of scholars and tourists alike.

THE LANDSCAPE

The importance of Italy in the ancient world is explained by her geographical position. The country juts out into the centre of the Mediterranean Sea, connected to continental Europe and also in contact with the countries of the eastern Mediterranean. Italy can be divided into two distinct regions, the northern continental and the central and southern peninsular; in addition there are the islands including Sicily (Fig. 1). Continental Italy consists of the great northern plain through which runs the river Po. The plain is bounded to the north by the high Alps and to the south by the northern Apennines. The Alps sweep in a semi-circle from the Dalmatian coast in the east to the Ligurian coast, where they join the Ligurian Apennines in the west. Contact with the rest of Europe was possible even in ancient times through the passes of this Alpine barrier, particularly the Brenner and the Little St. Bernard, as well as by the sea routes. From the northern plain the Apennines form a backbone down the length of peninsular Italy. These mountains can be crossed fairly easily at a number of passes. The eastern Apennines border a narrow coastal plain with few natural harbours. The western coastline which has been subject to many changes of level is more complicated; in the north the mountains sweep right down to the sea, further south in Tuscany foothills form hill masses and here the country's main metal deposits are found. These were exploited from an early date. Elba was a major source of iron, and on the mainland copper, iron and small quantities of tin were found in the Colline Metallifere and the region of the Tolfa hills. The same area was thickly forested providing wood for the smelting furnaces. The hinterland of Campania was very fertile and for this reason its ownership was constantly contested. Further south in Calabria and Apulia there were also rich farmlands, these together with reasonable harbours attracted the Greek colonists.

CHRONOLOGY AND TERMINOLOGY

The standard terms Palaeolithic, Mesolithic, Chalcolithic, Bronze and Iron signifying technological stages, still provide the basic chronological framework for Italian prehistory. As so many excavations are of cemeteries, rather than settlements where the successive occupation provides a relative sequence, divisions within these periods and from one area to another are still very uncertain. Slowly radiocarbon dating (obtained by measuring the radioactive disintegration of a carbon isotope, 'C14', present in all organic matter) is providing a series of absolute dates, which will eventually amount to a reliable chronological framework for each major period and for the various regions of Italy. For the present only very broad datings may be offered for the earliest periods.

4

Fig. 1

Although a chronological framework is vital for even the simplest examination of cause and effect in human history, the archaeologist needs also to organise his evidence in social terms. Recurrent associations of distinctive artefacts, burial customs, building styles, etc. are termed 'cultures' by archaeologists, sometimes named after the site where any one group of such characteristics was first identified. For instance, in the 1850s G. Gozzadini excavated a large number of graves, which he correctly interpreted as earlier than those of the historical Etruscans, in the vicinity of his vast personal estate of Villanova, near the north Italian town of Bologna (Etruscan Felsina). This gave its name to the Early Iron Age 'Villanovan' culture. The same type of burial and grave offerings were found over a wide area of Italy. Possession of a common material culture has inevitably given rise to the term 'Villanovans': but it should never be forgotten that this word is an illegitimate ethnic extrapolation from the modern description of an archaeological culture—unlike the ethnic term 'Etruscans', used by ancient writers to describe the non-Greek and non-Roman inhabitants of the area between the Tiber and the Arno.

SUMMARY CHRONOLOGICAL TABLE

The dates are approximate, especially so for the earlier periods

6000 BC	Neolithic
3000	Chalcolithic
2000	Early Bronze Age
1600	Middle Bronze Age
1300	Recent Bronze Age
1200	Final Bronze Age
900	Iron Age, (Villanovan culture)
720	The Orientalising Period
600	The Archaic Period
470	The Classical Period
323 (the death of Alexander the Great, to 30 BC)	The Hellenistic Period.

6

II The Neolithic Period—Stone Age

Farming and stockraising spread to Italy from the lands of the east Mediterranean. It has been increasingly recognised, however, that an important role in this process was played by the indigenous Mesolithic inhabitants, and a complex picture is emerging in which some areas developed rapidly and others changed only slowly after the first introduction of these new resources possibly before the sixth millennium BC. In general north and central Italy changed more slowly than the south east.

The earliest pottery-using groups, the makers of so-called impressed ware (pots decorated before firing with impressions jabbed in the soft clay with bone tools, shells or finger tips), were probably the descendants of the local Mesolithic hunting population who continued to live in caves or coastal sites gathering shells and simply keeping a few domestic sheep. These they obtained from farmers across the sea in Greece. Such an economy survived for millennia, especially in the north. Cereal-growing began earliest in the areas most closely in contact with the other side of the Adriatic Sea, and this arable farming is reflected in the settled villages of Apulia, with painted pottery of the kind common in the Balkans. The best evidence for these villages is found on the Tavoliere in Apulia.

The dry climate of the Tavoliere, a low-lying area of undulating farmland, bounded to the west by the foothills of the Apennines and lying inland from the Gulf of Manfredonia, accentuates the traces of ancient ditches cut through the calcareous crust just below the dark surface soil. These ditches show up in a remarkable way, particularly from the air. The area provides a unique opportunity to study Neolithic farming communities, an established economy rather different from the slowly changing communities in the north. Over a thousand sites, some single farms, others quite large villages, have been pinpointed by aerial photography. One of the pioneers of aerial photography in Italy was John Bradford, later of the Pitt Rivers Museum, Oxford. From the photographs he studied whilst serving with the allied forces in 1945 he identified many sites, some of which he was later able to examine on the ground. The largest village he investigated was Passo di Corvo (about seven miles north east of Foggia), the earliest 'C14' date from which is of the fifth millennium BC (Pl. I). Recent excavations have recorded over a hundred small compounds within each of which would have stood a round hut made of wattle and daub. These hut enclosures were surrounded by a double or triple ditch, beyond which a large area was enclosed either for cultivation or for animals. Stock would have been limited on the Tavoliere by the lack of water during the long hot summer months. Crops of corn were grown and stone querns for grinding the harvested grain have been found. Knives were sometimes made

7

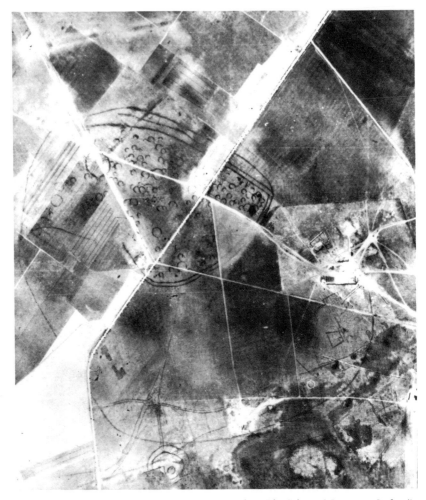

Plate I: Aerial view of Passo di Corvo (copyright Pitt Rivers Museum, Oxford).

of imported obsidian, black volcanic glass, but the most common material for tools was flint, readily obtainable from the nearby Gargano, a limestone promontory jutting out into the Adriatic Sea. Quantities of pottery fragments were collected of both impressed and painted wares and a selection from Passo di Corvo and other south eastern Neolithic sites has been given to the Museum by Mrs Bradford.

The earliest villages in the north are associated with square-mouthed pottery, a type which eventually spread over most of northern Italy and has been found even in Sardinia. At one of the sites where square-mouthed

8

vases were discovered, Molino Casarotto, the traces of rectangular wooden huts built on platforms by the lakeside have been found. Bones of wild animals, deer and boar, and of a very few domestic animals come from the rubbish thrown out from the huts, and quantities of fish bones and molluscs show that the lake was an important source of food. Some crops were grown and even grape pips have been identified. Obsidian, a material found on many sites throughout Italy, was used very effectively for tool-making. There were various sources of obsidian, Lipari, the Pontine Islands and Sardinia, each supplying a particular area. This seems to be clear evidence of commercial activity.

III The Chalcolithic Period—Copper Age

Most of the Neolithic sites were abandoned before the succeeding Copper Age (Chalcolithic) generally held to date from the third millennium BC. This period was characterised by many different cultures (Fig.2). There was a great increase in population and in technological expertise. Copper

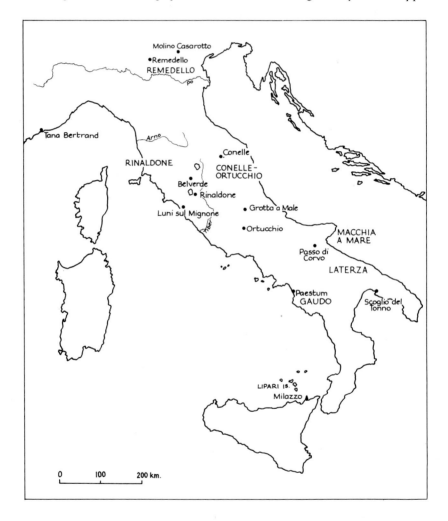

Fig. 2

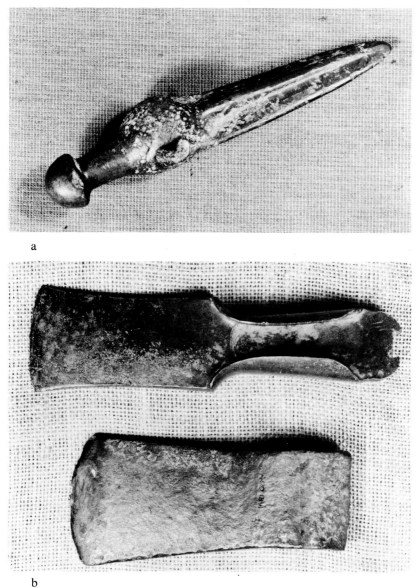

a

b

Plate II: *a*. Copper halberd macehead, from Santa Fiora, Monte Amiata, Tuscany, John Evans Collection, L. 0.171 [1927.1428], Rinaldone Culture. *b*. Bronze shaft-hole axe, from Calabria, L. 0.17 [1891.400], Bronze winged axe, from Civita Castellana (Falerii), John Evans Collection, L. 0.225 [1927.1415], Protovillanovan.

11

objects which had been found occasionally during the Neolithic period became far more common, particularly in central Italy. Previously it had been thought that nomadic warriors carrying copper weapons, perhaps coming from the east, displaced the peaceful settled Neolithic farmer, and that a pastoralist economy resulted. It now seems clear that the Copper Age farmers were established on settled farms and concentrated on raising stock; the richer individuals possessed metal tools and weapons.

It is likely that, even at this early date, the metal ores of Tuscany and the southern Alps were being used. The greatest number of copper objects have been found in central Italy in graves of the Rinaldone culture, which takes its name from a cemetery in Umbria. Most of our knowledge of this and other cultures comes from cemeteries rather than settlements. The typical Rinaldone burial place was a grave in which a single body was placed, but in some areas rock-cut tombs have been found with multiple burials. Besides the copper tools and weapons sometimes found (Pl. IIa), flint arrow- and spear-heads, stone tools and weapons and highly burnished dark brown clay bottles and cups were laid beside the body. The richest known Rinaldone site is at Belverde, where traces of food crops were found. Wheat, millet, barley, beans and perhaps grapes were grown. Sheep and goats were the most important domestic animals.

In the north of Italy the Remedello culture of the central plain was the most advanced, with strong connections with continental Europe. Flint weapons were the commonest grave gifts, but some copper axes and daggers and occasionally pots were placed beside the skeletons which were laid in a crouched position, in oval or rectangular graves.

In the north west the limestone caves of Liguria made ideal shelters and burial places for the Copper Age people. One cave, Tana Bertrand, was excavated by Mrs Crowfoot between 1907-1909, after she had discovered human bones whilst searching for the blind beetles which were said to live in the cave. Parts of at least ten skeletons and worked flints, stone beads, pendants and flakes of boar tusks were discovered (Pl. III). In some Ligurian cave-settlements fragments of Beaker pottery have been found of a type well-known in the rest of Europe. Beakers also come from open settlements and burials, mostly concentrated in the north of Italy in Chalcolithic and Early Bronze Age contexts. Some beakers are of different European styles, providing interesting evidence for contact with a number of different areas. Others seem distinctively Italian.

The Gaudo culture, named after a cemetery near Paestum in Campania, was clearly connected with the Rinaldone culture to the north. Flint weapons were the usual grave goods but many highly burnished brown vessels, mostly cups and *askoi*, multiple vases and a few copper objects have also been found. Other cultures (Conelle-Ortucchio), developed in the Marche and Abruzzi where settlements have been discovered. At the ditched settlement at Conelle, cattle, sheep and goat, red deer and a preponderance of swine bones have been identified. Villages have also been excavated on the Gargano promontory. Copper was rare here and further south where the Laterza culture flourished, characterised by pottery decorated with elaborate lattice and chevron patterns.

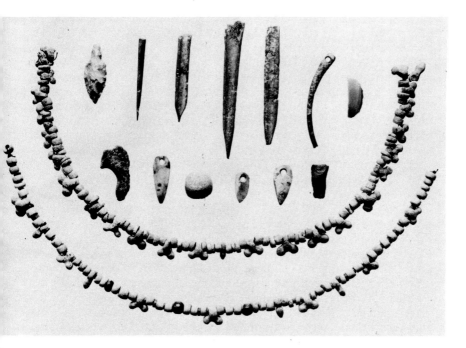

Plate III: Objects from the cave, Tana Bertrand, Badalucco, Liguria, given by Mrs Crowfoot, L. of longest string of beads 0.345 [1949.9ff], Chalcolithic.

IV The Bronze Age

The Bronze Age in Italy is conventionally divided into three phases. The Early Bronze Age (*c*. 2000—1600 BC) emerged with no very dramatic changes from the Copper Age, and a variety of cultures flourished. The Middle Bronze Age (*c*. 1600—1300 BC; Apennine and Terramare cultures) was a period of stability, during which settled communities prospered; the villages had contacts with other cultures, particularly to the south. The Late Bronze Age can be sub-divided into two phases, the Recent Bronze Age (*c*. 1300—1200) and the Final Bronze Age typified by the Proto-Villanovan culture (*c*. 1200—900). During the Recent Bronze Age the two most important cultures were the Sub-Apennine and Terramare, and a shift of emphasis in trade and influence from south to north can be traced. The Proto-Villanovan culture is characterised by urnfields which spread over a wide area of the peninsula.

The Apennine culture was dominant in central Italy in the Middle Bronze Age and by the Recent Bronze Age had spread until it stretched, with local differences, from the southern part of the Po plain to Calabria. Excavations at Luni sul Mignone (northern Latium) show a steady development of this flourishing culture. Traces of houses cut into the soft volcanic rock have been found and in the foundations sherds of 14th and 13th century Mycenaean pottery from Greece (p. 25). The Luni excavations give a picture of a settled community, whose economy was based on mixed farming. Faunal and plant samples have been analysed and carbonised wheat, barley, horse beans, pea grass and acorns have all been identified. The largest number of animal bones were those of cattle, sheep and goat; swine bones were found in lesser numbers. It is clear that domestic animals were important, and the farmers evidently exploited different pastures at various seasons and opened up new areas. The winters in the high Apennines would have been extremely cold, snow lying for several months, but by May the snows would have melted and lush grass have soon provided food for the animals brought up from the drought-stricken lowlands. By October the grass on the plains, fed by autumn rains, would have begun to grow again and the animals could be brought down to warmer winter pastures. Transhumance (seasonal movement of stock) became important in solving the problem of animal husbandry in a difficult climate. Sites have been found high up in the hills; one such is a huge cave, Grotta a Male, which started life as a shepherd's encampment, but had become a permanent settlement by the Recent Bronze Age.

The pottery of the Apennine culture appears to reflect the importance of domestic animals; a considerable number of so-called milk-boilers, believed in fact to have been used for making cheese, have been found, the

14

type varying from region to region. The characteristic Apennine pottery was dark burnished, decorated with hatched and dotted bands, spirals and maeanders. Carinated bowls with a single handle were very popular; later, particularly in the Sub-Apennine culture, the potters were to specialise in making elaborate handles, for these and other vessels.

There is ample evidence of contact with other peoples. The Mycenaean civilisation of Greece flourished from c. 1600 BC. During the fourteenth century trade played an important part and merchandise, particularly pottery, was exported to many Mediterranean areas including Italy. Mycenaean pottery fragments have been found as far north as Luni sul Mignone in central Italy, further south on the islands of Ischia and Vivara, at sites on the Tyrrhenian coast, and commonly in Apulia, the Aeolian Islands and Sicily. It has even been suggested that Mycenaean traders settled at such sites as Scoglio del Tonno. After the collapse of the Mycenaean empire in the 12th century BC there was a shift of trade and the Apennine people looked northwards, particularly to the Terramare culture of west Emilia.

The Terramare culture takes its name from the term used by local farmers in the nineteenth century to describe the mounds of black earth which they used for fertiliser. These mounds were composed of debris from Bronze Age settlements. Many of the Terramare villages were quite large, the people practising mixed farming. They grew wheat and other crops and raised cattle and sheep. Finds of red deer and wild boar bones, however, show that hunting was still important. A great variety of bronze tools and personal ornaments, including pins and combs, have been found, many showing influence from north of the Alps. Cremation was the common burial rite.

Cremation was the exclusive burial rite of a culture of the Final Bronze Age known, since 1939, as Proto-Villanovan. Discoveries since the last war have greatly increased our knowledge of this culture and recent excavations of sites scattered throughout Italy from Milazzo in Sicily to the Alps in the north have shown it to be complex. It can no longer be regarded simply as a short transitional phase between the Bronze Age and the Early Iron Age Villanovan Culture, for it lasted from about the thirteenth to the tenth century BC, overlapping with other Bronze Age and Early Iron Age cultures. It inherited some earlier elements, but it is clear that it was also open to new influences.

The form of cremation employed in the Proto-Villanovan period involved placing the ashes in a jar of coarse, badly fired pottery (*impasto*), which was made in a variety of shapes. This jar or urn was buried usually in a well-like pit grave (*tomba a pozzo*). Many such graves were crowded together in so-called urnfields. Simple bronze grave goods such as brooches (*fibulae*) of violin-bow type were placed in the urn with the ashes. Later a serpentine shape fibula was developed and rectangular razors were also popular. Some habitation sites have also been investigated, ranging from open villages composed of a few crude huts to quite large villages, almost towns. Several of the villages were built on well fortified hilltops chosen for their natural defences. The villagers would have practised mixed farming with an emphasis on stock rearing.

Hoards of metal work, bronze tools, weapons and vessels, have been found belonging to this phase (Pl. IIb). This suggests that merchants or itinerant metalsmiths visited the villages trading their wares. Some of the objects were new, others had been used or broken. Usually they vary in date, some showing connections with the Aegean world, others with cultures north of the Alps.

V The Early Iron Age

The major technological advance of the Bronze Age had been the addition of tin to copper to make an alloy which was harder than pure copper and easier to work. In the Early Iron Age iron was used only rarely, although the ores existed on the island of Elba and in Etruria. This metal, however, is not easy to work and in spite of its advantages over bronze the potential of the material was not fully exploited until the eighth century, when new techniques were learnt, probably from the Greeks.

Several different Iron Age cultures have been recognised, which can be divided into two main groups, on the basis of their burial customs: the inhuming cultures found in southern Italy and up the Adriatic coast and the cremating cultures found in northern Italy, Tuscany and in parts of Umbria and Latium.

THE VILLANOVAN CULTURE

The most advanced Early Iron Age culture c. 900-720 BC is now known as Villanovan after the hamlet of Villanova near Bologna where the 'type' cemetery was excavated by Count Gozzadini. Under his direction a great number of graves, nearly all cremations, was uncovered in the 1850s. Similar cremation graves have also been found in Tuscany, northern Latium and at Capua, Pontecagnano and Sala Consilina in Campania (an area where inhumation was the normal rite). To the east, in Picenum, another inhuming area, a cemetery has been excavated at Fermo with Villanovan-type graves.

In the north the culture developed slowly and continued into the sixth century BC when Etruscan influence became dominant. In central Italy the situation was rather more complex, since outside influences forced spectacular changes particularly in the later eighth century BC. Here two main phases evolved, Villanovan I c. 900-800 BC and Villanovan II c. 800-720 BC.

Although the preceding Proto-Villanovan culture of the Final Bronze Age shared many characteristics with Villanovan the question as to whether there was continuity between them is complex and not fully resolved. The Villanovan villages were at first built on low hills within easy reach of the sea and navigable rivers, but later also on the coastal plains. Most of our knowledge comes from the cemeteries, one reason being that settlements were often built over later by the Etruscans. This continuity between Villanovan villages and Etruscan towns has led many scholars to see the Villanovan culture as an early phase of the Etruscan.

The cemeteries were composed of well tombs (Fig. 3a), the ashes and partially burnt bones being placed in a biconical urn made of *impasto* (Pl. IVa); a bowl over the mouth served as a lid. In some men's graves a

b

Plate IV: *a*. Biconical *impasto* urn, from Veii, S. G. Owen bequest, H. 0.304 [1940.83]. *b*. Clay model helmet, used as an urn cover, H. 0.26 [1970.592], Villanovan.

a

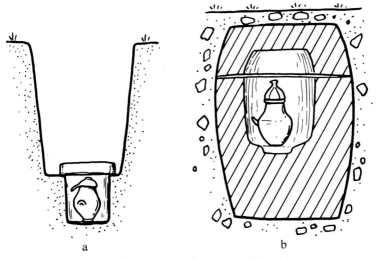

Fig. 3: Diagram of Villanovan well tombs.

clay model helmet replaced the bowl (Pl. IVb, Fig. 3b). The ash container and cover were sunk into the well tomb which was sometimes lined with small stones, or more elaborately with stone slabs. The urn was decorated with patterns; swastikas, maeanders and squares drawn with a comb-like tool. Occasionally the decoration was picked out with metal strips, most of which have now disintegrated leaving a white ghost pattern, as can be seen on the helmet illustrated (Pl. IVb). During Villanovan I iron objects

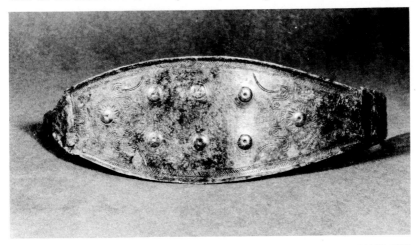

Plate V: Sheet bronze belt, given by the Rev. G. J. Chester, W. 0.101 [1890.619], Villanovan II.

19

a

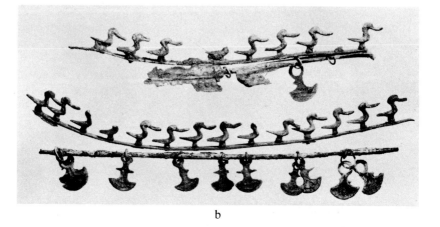

b

Plate VI: *a*. Bronze flask, given by Mr J. Bomford, D. 0.215 [1967.1069]. *b*. Parts of a bronze 'tray', from Lezoux, Puy-de-Dôme, France, given by Sir John Evans. L. of longest piece 0.36 [Pr.329-331], Villanovan II.

were very rare. The usual grave goods were small clay vases, simple bronze brooches, razors and rings.

In the eighth century (Villanovan II) a wider distribution of settlements and expanding foreign contacts reflected the general increase in prosperity. Men's graves contained bronze armour and horse trappings—bits and harness ornaments—as well as small personal articles such as brooches and lunate razors. In the women's graves were found necklaces of glass and amber, elaborate brooches, spindles and broad bronze belts, some decorated with birds and sun disks, patterns considered to be derived from Central Europe (Pl. V). Richly decorated sheet metal vessels have also been found including a 'pilgrim flask' (Pl. VIa). The advances in metalworking reflect changes in society. The apparently egalitarian system of the ninth and early eighth century seems to have broken down with the increase in prosperity and in the last decades of the eighth century a 'princely' or wealthy 'merchant' class emerged. Evidence for which has been found in chamber tombs with elaborate and varied objects which contrast strangely with the simple cremation burials that still continued. Inhumation was adopted gradually and then not in all regions. At first the body was laid out in a trench with spaces hollowed out for the grave goods. The trenches later became more elaborate and developed into the chamber tombs. The basis of the economy was agriculture, but the source of wealth was metal. Iron became increasingly used and hastened changes in tool-making so important for the expansion of agriculture. Some changes were certainly due to the influence of the earliest Greek colonists in Campania, where there were Villanovan-type cemeteries.

THE LATIAL CULTURE

Between the Villanovan peoples of Etruria and Campania lay Latium. The Iron Age culture of Latium drew its inspiration from the Villanovan culture to the north and the Fossa culture to the south, whilst at the same time developing its own particular character. The first Latial Period, tenth to early ninth century BC, corresponds roughly to the Proto-Villanovan stage of the Final Bronze Age and the early Villanovan stage of the Iron Age. In Latium, unlike further north, there is ample evidence of continuity between the Bronze Age sites and those of the Iron Age. Little is known of the scattered villages and most of our knowledge comes from the cemeteries. At first cremation was the usual rite. One type of ash container was the model hut urn (Pl. VII), which probably developed in the Alban Hills, which was an important centre. Small personal possessions of bronze such as rings and brooches were put with the ashes inside the urn. Fig. 4 shows the drawing of a hut urn burial in the Roman Forum. The hut had been put in a vast jar and surrounded by smaller jars and stands. The beginning of the full Iron Age, the Second Latial Period, dates from the first half of the ninth to the first half of the eighth century BC. Cremation continued as

Plate VII: Hut urn with cremated bones, from Monte Cucco, Alban Hills, given by Mr E. Oldfield, H. 0.311 [Pr.489], Latial Culture, *c*. 9th century BC.

Fig. 4: Drawing of Tomb Y in the Roman Forum, H. of the large jar in which the hut urn and other vases have been placed 0.575.

an important rite, but inhumation became increasingly popular with many different types of grave being used. This period saw considerable contact between Latium and Southern Etruria and many elements were common to both Villanovan and Latial cultures, particularly the small bronze grave goods. Variants of the model hut urn were also used in Etruria. The hut urn gives a very good impression of the homes of these Early Iron Age people: the real huts would have been made of wattle and daub and thatched. A drawing (Fig. 5) shows the reconstructed framework of a hut

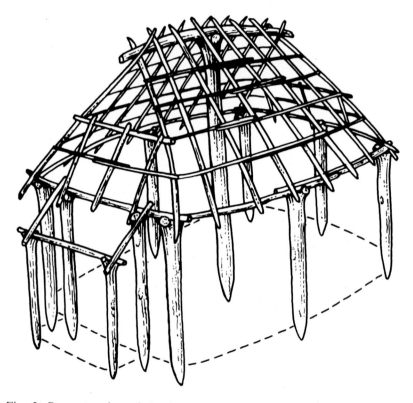

Fig. 5: Reconstruction of the framework of Hut A on the Palatine, Rome, L. 4.90, W. 3.60. Early Iron Age.

on the Palatine Hill, in one of the villages which were eventually to emerge as the city of Rome. These villages were beginning to grow in importance at the expense of those on the Alban Hills. The excavators on the Palatine found holes in the ground left by wooden posts, long since rotted away, and were able to plot the ground plan of the huts. Other huts and houses have recently been investigated at Tarquinia and at Ficana near Rome.

The difference between the Latial and Villanovan cultures widened as inhumation became more and more popular in Latium. Trench tombs were often enclosed by a stone circle, a custom which spread to the Faliscan area. There is a great deal of evidence that contacts increased between the peoples of Latium, and the 'Villanovans' and the peoples of the Fossa culture in Campania. By the middle of the eighth century BC, the Third Latial Period, the influence of the Greek colonists on Ischia and mainland Cumae became apparent.

EARLY CONTACTS WITH THE GREEKS AND PHOENICIANS

Already in the ninth century the 'Villanovans' in Etruria were using the regional metal ores and were accomplished metal-workers. Greek merchants knew the area and were presumably well aware of the region's potential as a source of metal. Recent finds of imported Greek pottery in Etruria, Latium and Campania have shown that commercial relations existed between the Greeks and the inhabitants of central Italy before the foundation of the first Greek colonies Greek two-handled drinking cups decorated with a band of chevrons (chevron *skyphoi*) have been found at several sites including Capua, Cumae and Pontecagnano in Campania and Veii in Etruria These cups predate the earliest colonies and this suggests 'trade before the flag'. It is more than likely that the Euboeans of Eretria and Chalkis chose Pithekoussai on the island of Ischia just off the Campanian coast as the site of the first Greek colony (*c.* 770 BC), because it provided a secure base for trading. They probably could not settle nearer to the metal-producing area in Etruria because the 'Villanovans' were firmly established on land, and 'Villanovan' sailors or pirates (the line must have been hard to draw) controlled the sea locally This would argue fairly sophisticated institutions organising trade and defence. Phoenician colonisers who doubtless were also interested in the metals of Etruria, were unable to establish a colony nearer than Sardinia. In the Odyssey of Homer the Phoenicians are portrayed as makers of, and traders in, precious goods, dealing in small trinkets and luxury objects, buying in one place, selling in another.

The Euboeans had established Al Mina in Syria as a trading centre in the east, and Pithekoussai and Cumae were the western counterparts There can be little doubt that the first colonists were primarily interested in trading for metal. Iron slag found on Ischia has been shown by analysis to come from Elba. The discovery of crucibles encrusted with iron and the clay mouths of bellows used for fanning the furnaces is further proof of metal-working. Bronze and lead were also worked on the island. The colonies became centres for the diffusion of ideas and objects. There is evidence at Pithekoussai from *c.* 740 BC of resident Orientals. Many of the surviving traded objects were trinkets, such as the seals of the so-called

O   1 CM.

Fig. 6: Drawing of impression of a seal of the 'Lyre Player Group', a double-headed figure flanked by plants, from the necropolis of Montarano, Falerii. Third quarter of the eighth century BC.

'Lyre Player Group' (Fig. 6) made in north Syria and found in children's graves on Ischia and also in Etruria. Such objects give a foretaste of the great number of exotic pieces from a variety of east Mediterranean sources found in Etruria, Latium and Campania in the later eighth century. The Orientalising influence owed a lot to the stimulus of both Euboean merchants and Phoenician traders. There is occasional evidence for goods moving the other way. Villanovan fibulae are found at Pithekoussai and were probably copied there, and a bronze belt of Villanovan II type (cf. Pl. V) is believed to have reached Euboea itself. A bronze bit decorated with horses has been found at Olympia. An interesting example of a Villanovan export, west across the Alps, is provided by parts of a bronze 'tray' decorated with rows of little ducks and dangling pendants from Lezoux in France (Pl. VIb). Such trays are found in graves of north Italy and sometimes in Etruria.

Greek vases were soon copied by 'native' potters (Pl. VIII). These two illustrated vases decorated with geometric patterns in red paint were found near Capua: others of the same type come from Etruria and the Faliscan area. The early influence of the Euboean craftsmen was replaced at the end of the eighth century by Corinthian inspiration. Corinthian vases were imported and also copied at Pithekoussai (Pl. XIII) where there were important clay beds. They were extremely popular in Etruria and Latium, and later the Etruscan potters were to set up workshops copying Corinthian products.

One of the most important contributions of the Greek colonists, which shows the closeness of Cumaean contacts with Etruria, is the transmission of the alphabet to the Etruscans and Latins. One might have thought that the Etruscans would have borrowed their letters directly from the Phoenicians who visited their ports, but this seems not to have happened. The Etruscan alphabet can be shown to have derived from the western form of Greek alphabet, that used by the Chalcidians of Euboea.

The sea route up the Tyrrhenian coast was one way by which the Greek and other merchants could have traded their wares, but many traders preferred one of the land routes running north from Campania. One road ran to the west of the Lepini mountains and Corinthian vases and their copies have been found at sites lying along this route, Satricum, Lavinium, Castel di Decima and Rome. A second land route lay to the east of the mountains up the valleys of the Sacco and Liri rivers emerging at Palestrina (Praeneste) a leading settlement in the Tiber valley. Whichever route was chosen the Tiber had to be crossed to reach the metal-producing areas of Etruria. There were several crossing places but the lowest was at Rome.

Plate VIII: Globular vase and cup with geometric decoration in red paint, from near Capua, given by Dr C. M. Kraay, H. 0.22; 0.085 [1958.68-9], restored. 8th century BC.

PICENE AND OTHER EARLY IRON AGE CULTURES

The inhabitants of Etruria also traded across the Apennines eastwards and the Villanovan culture spread to Fermo, a cemetery in sight of the Adriatic Sea, in the region known to the Romans as Picenum (Marche and part of the Abruzzi). The Picene culture flourished from the ninth century and was concentrated largely in an area between the rivers Foglia and Pescara, a narrow strip of land cut by river valleys leading to the Adriatic Sea, and bounded to the west by the Apennine mountain range. Archaeologists have divided the culture found in this area into several phases. In Picene I (ninth century BC) grave goods were extremely simple, consisting of small clay vases whose elaborate handles seem to show Sub-Apennine influence, and bronze brooches with a disc foot or simple arched bow and catchplate. Except at Fermo where the bodies were cremated and the ashes placed in the usual Villanovan biconical urn, the dead were laid in a crouched position in trench graves. This method of burial continued into the following century (Picene II), when the graves held a much wider variety of offerings, including distinctive locally made objects such as a bronze pin with folded head, as well as many Villanovan-type gifts, and spectacle fibulae introduced from across the Adriatic Sea. In the later eighth century little animal pendants became popular and the objects became more fussy with dangling pendants and droplets. Many pieces were decorated with amber such as the fibula illustrated (Fig. 7). Picenum was probably a centre for amber traded from the Baltic. Much of the

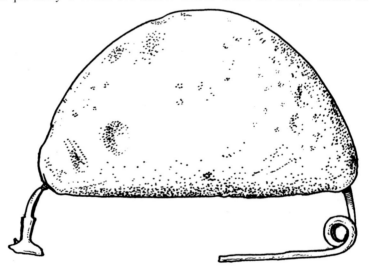

Fig. 7: Bronze fibula, part of the pin missing, a large piece of amber is threaded through the bow, L. 0.095 [1890.2], 7th century BC.

28

Plate IX: Small bronzes, previously restored as a wheeled cart, from Lucera, Apulia, given by Mr W. M. Wylie, H. of greatest 0.255 [1836-68 Catalogue, p.19]. 7th century BC.

translucent fossil resin was re-exported to Etruria and Apulia, either made into attractive ornaments or as raw material.

In Apulia some of the open villages had developed into small heavily fortified towns as early as the thirteenth century BC. It seems likely that trade was a major factor in the growth of these early settlements. Bronze, a material not found in the south, was brought from the north and quantities of Mycenaean sherds testify to trade with the Aegean. Early in the Iron Age there were several groups of people practising inhumation in Apulia and each group developed its own particular type of painted pottery. Even before the arrival of the Greek colonists the potters were copying patterns taken from Greek vases, and by about 725 BC regional schools developed (later examples are illustrated Fig. 16).

The Ashmolean has several little bronze figures of wiry men, ducks and other animals; they include deer surmounting wheels (Pl. IX). These were found at Lucera (Apulia) in the last century and restored as a wheeled cart. They are typical of the elaborate bronzes in the area. Spectacle fibulae and pendants were also popular.

After the foundation of the Greek colonies along the coast of Messapia, there came a second series, offspring of the first, strung out along the western coast of Calabria and Lucania, although not along the east coast of Apulia. Thus 'a Greek fringe was woven around the coasts of the Barbarian' (Cicero de Rep. II.iv.9), (Fig. 8). Southern Italy was turned into Magna Graecia and Sicily became a Greek island.

The growth of the colonies cut short the development on separate lines of the cultures neighbouring the Greek cities. Research has concentrated

29

on the colonies and the goods made in them by Greek craftsmen. Recently excavations and surveys have sought to discover the relations of the colonists with their 'native' neighbours, the extent of trade and influence and even settlement of the Greeks within the native villages.

Fig. 8

VI The Early Etruscans

The Villanovan culture had shown a remarkable degree of uniformity, particularly in the ninth century BC, and had developed without a break until the end of the eighth century. This gradual development continued in the north round Bologna for a further two centuries, but there was a great upsurge in prosperity to the south, in the area bounded by the rivers Arno and Tiber, the region known as Etruria (modern Tuscany, western Umbria and northern Latium). Changes in society are indicated by the emergence of a 'princely' class, whose members were buried in chamber tombs with precious objects brought from many different lands, and by the amalgamation of villages and small towns into sizeable cities. It is at this point that the people long known to us as the Etruscans are first recorded in this region. Were they newcomers from across the sea or were they just newly prosperous 'Villanovans' under another name?

The debate is as old as history. Herodotus writing in the fifth century BC tells how the kingdom of Lydia endured a famine for eighteen years under the king Atys: 'still the affliction continued and even became more grievous. So the king determined to divide the nation in half, and to make the two portions draw lots, the one to stay the other to leave the land'. The losers set sail from Smyrna under the king's son Tyrrhenus and reached Italy where they settled and founded cities. The 'invasion' by the Lydians is meant to have taken place shortly after the Trojan War. This was the prevalent view until the first century BC when the historian Dionysius of Halicarnassus reviewed all the available evidence and decided on balance that the Etruscans were an indigenous Italian people.

In spite of the changes, the material remains do seem to show a continuous development, and to stress the continuity between the 'Villanovans' and the Etruscans some scholars use the terms Archaic I and II instead of Villanovan I and II, and Archaic III to indicate the rise of the Etruscan city states.

THE ORIENTALISING PERIOD (ARCHAIC III, *c.* 720-600 BC)

By the end of the eighth century the eastern goods in some tombs were superlatively rich and this has led other scholars to call this phase the Orientalising Period. The oriental objects did not all come from one source and the most likely explanation for their presence is trade with various areas. The most common current view, based on the archaeological evidence, is that the Etruscan culture evolved over a long period from the Villanovan which was subjected to considerable influence from trade and traders. An enormous part would have been played by the Greek colonies, stimulating

31

new ideas and bringing in goods, and there is considerable evidence too for Phoenician traders. The ores of Etruria were the targets of the merchants, and were doubtless the reason for its dominant position amongst the Italic regions. Recent excavations, however, have shown that Etruria was not the only area to enjoy an Orientalising phase. The fourth Latial Period (late 8th-7th century BC) corresponds to the Orientalising Period in Etruria. The Bernadini and Barberini tombs at Palestrina have been known for a long time, there were rich tombs at Tivoli, and recently the discoveries at Castel di Decima, many of earlier date, have produced quantities of Orientalising material. In Picenum the Orientalising tombs of Fabriano and Pitino di S. Severino were filled with exotic objects collected from many sources.

The most advanced area in Etruria was the south, where the great cities of Tarquinia, Cerveteri, Veii and Vulci developed These towns doubtless controlled trade. As a general rule the northern and inland cities, such as Vetulonia and Chiusi, lagged a little behind, often retaining old traditions. Etruscan towns were also established at Capua and elsewhere in Campania, and at centres on the trade routes lying between Campania and Etruria, such as Palestrina and Rome. The outlying towns in Campania may have been developed at the same time as the main Etruscan centres, rather than, as had once been thought, at a later date and by Etruscan colonists The wealth of the cities is reflected in the goods found in the cemeteries. Many of the most important burials were in chamber tombs, in a style which no doubt reflected domestic building practices of the day An elaborate chamber tomb normally had a long entrance passage leading into a rect-angular antechamber surrounded by side rooms and at the end a burial chamber. The roof was made of overlapping stones, often the whole was covered by an enormous mound or tumulus. More than one chamber tomb could be built beneath the mound.

The early Orientalising tombs held an amazing variety of goods: bronze cauldrons decorated with griffin and lion heads, gold jewellery, silver dishes, ivory vessels and ornaments, faience amulets and flasks, ostrich eggs and tridacna shells. Objects imported from Greece, north Syria, Phoenicia, Egypt, and perhaps Crete and Cyprus were placed with locally made vases and bronzes as grave goods. Some objects would have been made by groups of immigrant craftsmen, and may be indistinguishable from imported goods. Soon the immigrants were teaching the native artists, who were peculiarly receptive to foreign influence, how to fashion the exotic materials. Their pupils, trained in foreign methods but retaining their own individuality, established their own style which can be called 'Etruscan Orientalising'. We can often see the influence that an imported object had on these artists, but it must also be remembered that some materials will have perished and these too would have introduced new motifs. In this respect textiles would have been of great importance. A late sixth-century Attic red figure cup, found in a tomb at Cerveteri, shows how elaborate

Fig. 9: Drawing of one of the Nereids from Side A. Herakles and Nereus, on an Attic red figure cup by Oltos, from Tomba Martini Marescotti, Cerveteri. Late sixth century BC.

patterned fabrics could be. The artist Oltos has painted a woman wearing a dress embroidered with delightful little animals (Fig. 9).

Local craftsmen copying the strange imports, or goods made by immigrants in unfamiliar materials, produced objects which to Eastern or Greek eyes would have appeared barbaric. A good example of such a piece comes from Tivoli in Latium and is a small ivory lion with a human victim (Pl. Xa). The raw ivory would have been imported probably from north Syria; unworked ivory has been found at Circolo della Costiaccia, Vetulonia. Other ivories from Tivoli of the same early period portray lions and horsemen ((Pl. Xb, c): a bracelet with lion-head terminals is decorated

a   b

c   d

Plate X: *a, b, c,* Ivories from near Tivoli. Lion with victim; two lions addorsed with victims; two confronted horsemen. H. 0.046, L. 0.042; H. 0.064; H. 0.06 (Pr.326, 325, 324). Early 7th century BC. *d.* Silver plaque with bronze backing, the 'Mistress of the Beasts' within a border of tiny heads. Formerly Bomford Collection. H. 0.06 [1976.38]. Later 7th century BC.

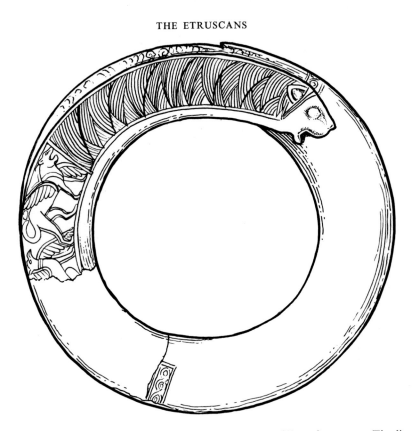

Fig. 10: Ivory arm-ring decorated with lions and griffins, from near Tivoli, D. 0.125 (Pr.323). First half of the seventh century BC.

with oriental designs, such as the file of animals and the cable decoration (Fig. 10).

The Etruscan artist relied on oriental motifs to develop his own style not only for carving ivories but also for decorating bronzes (Fig. 11), a field in which he was already highly skilled. Large bronze shields found in tombs were at first (in the early seventh century) decorated with geometric designs drawing on traditional 'Villanovan' patterns. Later (Pl. XI) a variety of oriental motifs were incorporated: palmettes, cables and files of sphinxes. The Tomba degli Scudi e Sede at Cerveteri, of slightly later date, shows how such shields, made in south Etruria, were hung in a tomb (Fig. 12). Palmettes were also used to decorate native pottery; an example of this can be seen on the white-on-red ware amphora (Pl. XIIa). A great school of jewellers developed, first in south Etruria, later in the north at Vetulonia, employing the technique of granulation: using tiny gold particles, to decorate brooches and other personal ornaments. A

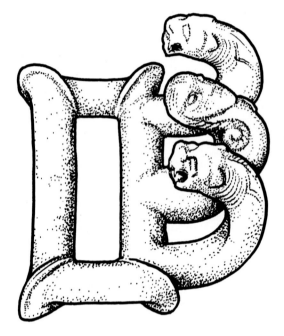

Fig. 11: Bronze belt buckle, the hooks in the form of a human head and two lion heads, formerly John Evans Collection, L. 0.067 [1927.1947]. 7th century BC.

silver plaque made in southern Etruria (Pl. X d) has a woman and palmette decoration. The woman has lion-head snake-like attachments and is probably inspired by the Phoenician Mistress of the Beasts. The same theme is used on bucchero ware, the Etruscan pottery which also evolved in the seventh century BC.

Bucchero ware was the most successful fabric produced by Etruscan potters. It was probably first made at Cerveteri, a town noted for other fine pottery. Another ware made there, decorated with 'herons' painted in red (Pl. XIIb), had a wide diffusion, even reaching Sicily. The clay used to make bucchero vases was refined, in contrast to the gritty clay of *impasto* vases from which bucchero ware developed. The pots were placed in a closed kiln, so that the reducing atmosphere fired the clay black or grey right through to the core. The black surface was often given a metallic sheen and many of the vase shapes seem to have been influenced by metalwork. The earliest Orientalising tombs contained no bucchero pottery, but by the middle of the seventh century it had become extremely popular. The earliest pots were of the highest quality with delicate thin walls (*bucchero sottile*) and careful decoration. The vase shapes were derived from a variety of sources: the amphora and kyathos (Fig. 13a, b) imitate earlier Italic vases; the tall necked jug (Fig. 13c) copies an oriental model; the skyphos (Fig. 13d) or drinking cup decorated with rays and fans derives from the Protocorinthian skyphos; a cup (Fig. 13e) is based on an East Greek shape. A shape, inspired by eastern ivory versions, which became extremely popular and persisted through the sixth century, was the chalice (Fig. 14a, b), either on a simple stemmed foot or supported by caryatids. Bucchero ware of the seventh and sixth century has been found at a number of sites ranging in the west from the Greek colonies of southern Italy and Sicily, Spain, Sardinia, southern France and Carthage to the Greek mainland and the islands in the east and to Asia Minor. The most popular shape exported was the kantharos (Fig. 13f). Later bucchero was, on the whole more clumsily made (p.   ).

THE LANGUAGE

Some bucchero vases have incised inscriptions. Although we do not know at what stage the Etruscan language was first being spoken, inscriptions have been found dating from the seventh century, written in the alphabet which had been introduced from the Greek colonies. Several thousand Etruscan inscriptions survive, nearly all of which are funerary, with short repetitive formulae, using a very limited vocabulary; the rest are dedications. One early inscription in the collection was discovered when an elaborately decorated bronze stand was cleaned. Decipherment is not a problem with Estruscan, for the words can be read: understanding the meaning of the words is quite another matter.

Fig. 12: Tomba degli Scudi e delle Sedie, Banditaccia necropolis, Cerveteri; shields in relief, approximately a metre in diameter, decorate the walls. C. 6th century BC.

Plate XI: Detail of a bronze votive shield. On loan from Lord Howard de Walden, D. 0.854. Late 7th century BC.

a

b

Plate XII: *a*. Red ware amphora decorated with birds and palmettes in white paint, H. 0.451 [1969.31]. *b*. Standed bowl, 'Heron Class'. Formerly Bomford Collection, H. 0.23 [1972.925]. 7th century BC.

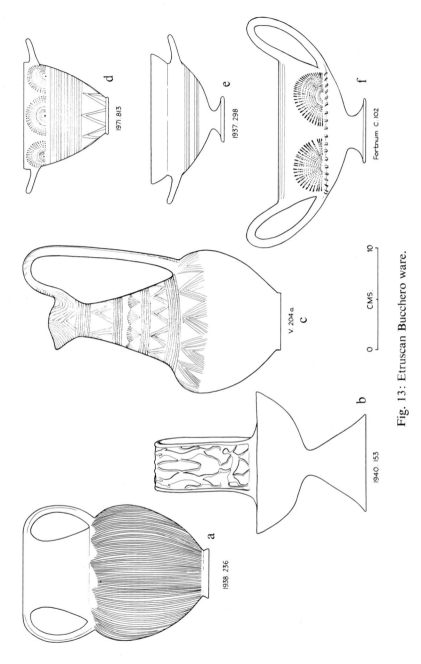

Fig. 13: Etruscan Bucchero ware.

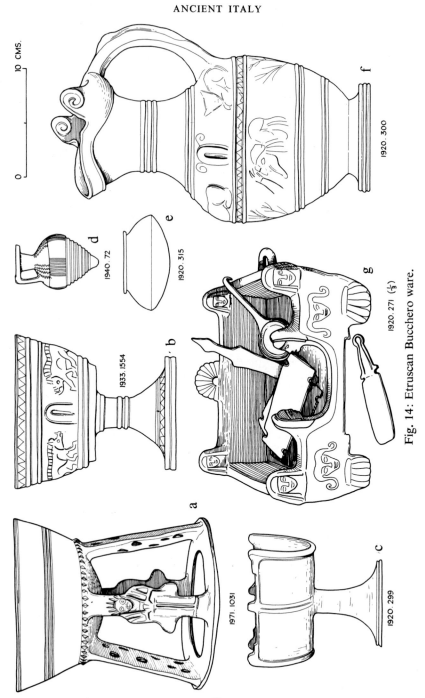

Fig. 14: Etruscan Bucchero ware.

10 CMS.

1920. 300   f

1940. 72   d

1920. 315   e

1920. 271 (⅓)   g

1933. 1554   b

1971. 1031   a

1920. 299   c

No Etruscan historical writing has survived: the only account we have of internal Etruscan politics is Livy's description (IV.60.g-V.I) of the debate which led to the refusal of aid by the other states to Veii at the end of the fifth century: a decision which led to the destruction of Veii in 396, and removed the final obstacle to Rome's inexorable advance into Etruria and Umbria.

ETRUSCAN EXPANSION

Because we have no written records it is impossible to reconstruct the political organisation of Etruria. By tradition the 'nation' comprised twelve city states. During the seventh century these cities were being established, built on the sites of the earlier villages. As one city rose to prominence another declined: various alliances were formed and commercial rivalries divided the states. Outside Magna Graecia the Etruscans are the only people in Italy (and indeed Europe) who can be held to have developed the city-state in pre-Roman times.

Although each area developed its own speciality dependent on the resources available, yet there was an overall general 'Etruscanisation'. By the end of the seventh century, the cities were looking outwards, far beyond the confines of Etruria, and Etruscan dominance was to spread from the Gulf of Salerno to the Alps. The extent of 'Etruscanisation' was by no means uniform and some areas even within the geographical territory of Etruria were to retain much of their independence. One such area was the *Ager Faliscus*, which lay in the river Treia drainage basin, bounded to the east by the Tiber and to the west by Lakes Bracciano and Vico. This was a volcanic region cut by deep gorges and high cliffs, which formed strong natural boundaries. In the eighth century the bronze goods placed in the cremation graves were strongly influenced by Villanovan types whereas the clay vases were more akin to those of Latium (see a grave group in the collection from Civita Castellana (*Falerii Veteres*)). The Faliscans also enjoyed an Orientalising period decorating their metalwork with fantastic animals and palmettes. In spite of the influence of Etruria, the Faliscans were able to retain their own language, speaking a local dialect of Latin. In the east in Picenum the people also retained their individuality in spite of Etruscan incursions.

To the south, Etruscan and Latial cultures were interwoven and in Rome the Tarquin dynasty was established at the end of the seventh century, and was to last for a hundred years. Etruscan expansion into Campania is supposed to have been by colonists who set up twelve city states based on the political system of the motherland. The most important town was Capua, but there is evidence of Etruscan presence in towns as far south as Sorrento and Pompeii. The exploitation of Campania led to new influences entering Etruria overland from the East Greek colony of Sybaris. During the sixth century Etruria, then an ally of Carthage, found herself involved in political struggles. The Phocaeans attempted to expand their colony at Alalia on Corsica. This posed a growing threat to the Etruscans on the mainland and the Carthaginian colonies on Sardinia. The alliance forced the Phocaeans to abandon Alalia (*c.* 535) and move south to the mainland, where Elea (Velia) was founded. The expansion to the south had brought Etruria into direct conflict with the Greek colonies and by 524 BC war broke out. Twenty years later at the battle of Aricia (*c.* 504 BC) the Latins allied with Aristodemus of Cumae defeated the Etruscans. Etruscan power was broken in Latium and land routes to Campania severely curtailed. Sybaris, which had been supplying Etruria with goods through Campania, was destroyed in 510 BC, and according to tradition the Etruscan king of Rome, Tarquinius Superbus, was expelled a year later. In 474 BC the Etruscans were defeated by Greek forces and their influence in Campania and Latium dwindled even further.

At the end of the sixth century, the political situation in the south led the Etruscans to concentrate more on the north. They were able to cross the Apennines to the Po valley, where, again, they are said to have founded twelve city states. The most important town was Bologna (Felsina) which became a vital link on the trade routes between Etruria and the north and the eastern port of Spina. Spina, at the mouth of the Po, developed as the major port, controlling the northern Adriatic, a meeting place of many cultures from the last quarter of the sixth century. Vast cemeteries have been excavated and the graves have yielded great quantities of imported Attic vases, as well as Italic and Etruscan goods. To the north west the Etruscans' way seems to have been barred by the Ligurians and to the north east the Veneti held sway, but Etruscan influence penetrated even these areas.

VII The Etruscans of the Archaic and Early Classical Periods

POTTERY

By the later part of the seventh century, the oriental styles began to lose their appeal and the growing influence of Greek pictorial art had begun. With the sixth century, Greek influence had become dominant. Black figured Corinthian vases had been exported in considerable numbers to Etruria and Latium as well as to the Greek colonies. The fabric was copied first in the colonies (Pl. XIII), and workshops were soon set up in Etruria itself, at Vulci, Cerveteri and Tarquinia, to meet the local demand. Some shapes were copied in bucchero ware (Fig. 14, d, e). The products of these potteries are called Etrusco-Corinthian and are often lively objects rather

Plate XIII: Aryballoi. Early Proto-Corinthian, from Cumae, given by Prof. Stuart Jones, H. 0.072 [1927.4595], c. 720-690 BC. Imitation of Proto-Corinthian, decorated with fish, from Cumae, formerly Vernon Collection, H. 0.061 [1927.7]. Early 7th century BC. Etrusco-Corinthian, decorated with a panther, by the Tree Painter, from Mancini's excavations at Orvieto, Mrs G. H. Pope bequest, H. 0.082 [1933.1562]. Early 6th century BC.

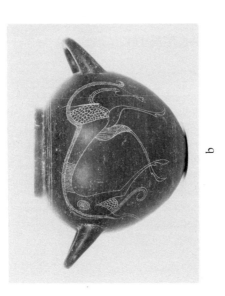

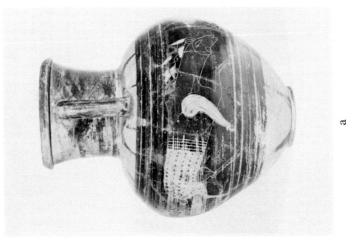

Plate XIV: *a.* Polychrome amphora decorated with fantastic animals, H. 0.334 [1971.909]. *b. Buccheroid impasto* jar, foot missing, decorated with an incised horse, H. 0.245 [1972.2001]. Both formerly Bomford Collection. 6th century BC.

than mere slavish copies. Most of the vases have no figures but are decorated with patterns. Some have animal friezes which often show the creatures clumsily drawn, sometimes with limbs dangling from their jaws. One type of ware in rather different style is called the Etruscan Polychrome Group (Pl. XIVa); the figures are drawn with incision on a solid black background and are picked out with colours. The result is amusing, the animal's bodies being patterned as if they were wearing brightly coloured rugs. The Etruscan's delight in animals is also seen in little perfume flasks (Pl. XV). This type of vase occurred frequently in the seventh and sixth centuries in Corinth, and the East Greek world and was exported to Etruria and imitated by the Etruscan potters.

A type of ware related to Etruscan Polychrome is the so-called *buccheroid impasto*, which is decorated with incised animals (Pl. XIVb); it is found mainly in the Capena region, the area south of the *Ager Faliscus* which was under Etruscan influence but retained some independence and spoke the Faliscan dialect.

By the middle of the sixth century imports of Attic black-figure vases were becoming more common and had a profound effect on the Etruscan potters. New styles arose under strong East Greek influence and it is more than likely that once again groups of immigrant craftsmen were instrumental in forming the new ideas. The style is found not only influencing the local schools of pottery but also the wall paintings in the rich tombs at

Plate XV: Perfume vases. A monkey holding a bowl, some restoration, from 'Cerri', Tuscany, H. 0.095 [1880.11, V.320a]. Hedgehog, H. 0.065, L. 0.090 [1923.389]. Swan, given by the Rev. G. J. Chester, H. 0.076 [1884.340]. Pig, L. 0.060 [1934.352]. Early 6th century BC.

Plate XVI: *a*. Chalcidian neck amphora by the Orvieto Painter, a symposium. Formerly Rycroft and Spencer-Churchill Collections, H. 0.282 [1965.132], third quarter of the 6th century BC. *b*. Pontic neck amphora, by the Paris Painter, riders, probably from Vulci. H. 0.338 [1961.529], c. 525 BC.

Tarquinia, the metalsmiths' workshops, and the studios making terracottas and jewellery.

During the sixth and early fifth centuries Etruria had strong connections with Greece, a fact that has been underlined recently by the results of excavations at Porto Clementino (*Gravisca*), the port of Tarquinia. These have revealed ample evidence of a Greek settlement. Cerveteri, a city of great importance, had a treasury at Delphi and was known to consult the oracle there in times of stress. Its cemeteries contained quantities of Attic black-figure vases. The so-called Caeretan *hydriai* (water jars) were quite possibly made in a workshop at Cerveteri. These splendid vases were heavily indebted both to East Greek workmanship and to Attic, yet they also reflect a number of purely Etruscan features. Cerveteri is also suggested as the home of Chalcidian black figure vases (Pl. XVIa), but much more problematically. Some of the vases have inscriptions written with the alphabet of Chalkis (hence the name). Vases of this type have all been found in the west, in Etruria, South Italy and Sicily. Corinthian and Attic influence is apparent and there is a strong East Greek element, but there seems nothing Etruscan in the style. Perhaps, therefore, Rhegium, a Chalcidian colony, is a more likely location for the pottery.

Another great city, Vulci, was to play a dominant role in Etruria. It had already been responsible for introducing Corinthian styles, and a particularly lively and attractive group of black figure vases found in Etruria was probably made there, for a large number of vases come from the city's necropolis, some beautifully made but others poorly fired and badly painted. Vases of the latter, slovenly type were unlikely to have been traded far. This ware has been given the name 'Pontic', since it was once thought to have been made at some Greek colony on the shores of the Black Sea. Several different painters working in this school have been identified by their style of painting, and since none have signed their work, archaeologists have given them conventional names. The founder of the school may have been the Paris Painter (Pl. XVIb), so-called from an amphora in Munich painted with a scene showing the Judgment of Paris. The Paris Painter started work about the middle of the sixth century and he and his followers continued production for about fifty years. The makers of Pontic vases drew inspiration for the decorative style, motifs and shape from a variety of sources. The East Greek (Ionian) influence has led many scholars to think that the pottery was established by an Ionian artist from overseas, but East Greek influence is not the only one discernible. The artists borrowed shapes from Attic models; it is also possible to trace Corinthian influence, but this may be through Etrusco-Corinthian wares rather than direct. There are complicated connections too with a whole range of other objects made in Etruria at this time, particularly impressed red ware made in Cerveteri (Pl. XVII), which has similar animals; bucchero ware; gold rings probably made by immigrant Greek artists (Pl. XVIII. a); architectural terracottas (Pl. XXII); and tomb paintings.

A type of black figure ware less lively than Pontic developed towards the end of the sixth century BC (Pl. XIXa). The leading artist, who was certainly Etruscan, was the Micali Painter, called after a nineteenth-century archaeologist. In the first half of the fifth century there were still many black figure vases being made, but most of these were of very poor quality and Etruscan artists began to imitate the Attic red figure vases which were being produced by about 530-520 BC. At first the Etruscans experimented with the use of red painted over the black background, a practice which was also used in the fourth century. The true red figure technique, in which patterns and figures were left in the red colour of the clay and the background filled with black did not begin in Etruria until the middle of the fifth century. It was not until the fourth century that this technique really gained ground and various schools developed.

Etruscan black figure artists seem to have influenced the work of Campanian painters perhaps centred at Capua (Pl. XIXb); the work of the two areas is sometimes confused. Etruscan influence can also be detected in the 'barbarous' imitations of Attic red figure vases (notably Nolan amphoras), of the so-called Owl Pillar Group, probably also made in Campania (Pl. XIXc).

Plate XVII: Large red ware 'brazier' with impressed decoration round the rim, a hare hunt, other animals and mythical creatures, D. c.0.57 [1971.938], 6th century BC.

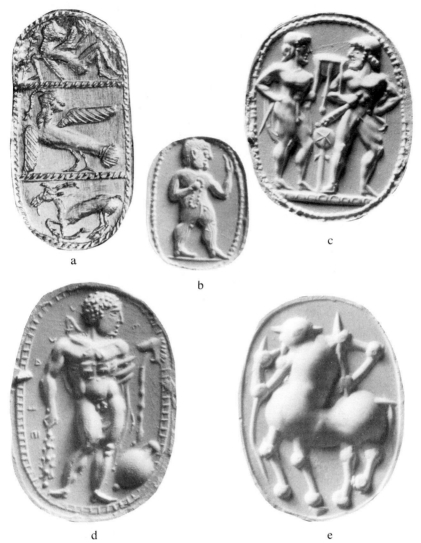

Plate XVIII: *a*. Gold and gilt silver ring, a winged figure, a siren, a goat, 16×8 mm. (Fortnum FR 52). Third quarter of 6th century BC. *b*. Agate scarab, a youth with wreath by the Master of the Boston Dionysos. From Tarquinia, 9×7 mm (Fortnum FR 74). Late 6th century BC. *c*. Cornelian scarab, Herakles and Apollo with the tripod. Formerly Spencer-Churchill Collection, 15×10 mm [1965.352]. First quarter of the 5th century BC. *d*. Cornelian scarab, Herakles at the fountain, inscribed. Formerly Story-Maskelyne Collection, given by Sir John Beazley, 16×11 mm [1921.1234]. Late 5th century BC. *e*. Cornelian scarab, centaur, 17×13 mm (Fortnum G.28). Late 4th or 3rd century BC.

51

a

b

c

Plate XIX: *a*. Etruscan black figure jug by the Micali Painter, a sphinx on either side, from Cerveteri, H. 0.22 [1937.160]. *b*. Campanian black figure amphora, a sphinx and birds, H. 0.232 [1937.163]. Both given by Sir John Beazley. *c*. Campanian amphora, the Owl Pillar Class, from Suessula, given by Prof. Stuart Jones, H. 0.28 [1927.4599]. 5th century BC.

The ties between Campania and Etruria weakened and by the fourth century Campanian vase painting had become part of the general South Italian scene. Colonists in Southern Italy began to make their own vases, rather than rely on Attic red figure imports, and different schools developed. By the beginning of the fourth century, five principal regional fabrics can be distinguished, Apulian, Lucanian, Campanian, Paestan and Sicilian; examples of these can be seen in the Beazley Room and the Sunken Court. Suprisingly, very little South Italian ware has been found in Etruria, although it had a profound influence in the area.

Bucchero ware still continued to be popular in the sixth and fifth centuries. As a general rule the later work was more clumsy, the walls thicker, the shapes less refined and the surface finish duller (*bucchero pesante*) (Fig. 14). Some bucchero vases were exported, particularly the kantharos, a two-handled drinking cup (Fig. 13f). Shapes of Etruscan bucchero ware were imitated in Athens, one example is the amphora which was copied by the potter Nikosthenes, who catered especially for the Etruscan market (Pl. XXa, b), and exported all his examples of this shape there. Human and animal friezes impressed with a roller stamp decorated many vases. The most important centres specialising in this technique were at Orvieto, Chiusi (Fig. 15), Cerveteri and Tarquinia.

Fig. 15: A procession scene from a fragment of a bucchero chalice with impressed cylinder decoration, given by Sir John Beazley. 0.11 × 0.065 [1966.1785]. 6th century BC.

Mould-made decoration was also used, particularly at the potteries at Chiusi (Fig. 14f), an inland town which grew in importance as the Etruscans expanded northwards. Chiusi was an area which was traditionalist, it had retained cremation as a burial rite long after other areas had turned to inhumation. The ashes were placed in urns with lids in the form of human heads. The urn, commonly called *canopic* from its supposed resemblance to Egyptian funerary jars, often stood on a pottery or bronze 'throne' and was then put in a very large jar and sunk into the ground (Pl. XXIa, b).

b

a

Plate XX: *a*. Attic black figure Nikosthenic amphora, a man courting a boy, from Cerveteri, H. 0.295 [1885.654, V.215], c. 530 BC. *b*. Etruscan bucchero Nikosthenic amphora. Formerly Bomford Collection, H. 0.325 [1971.937], Early 6th century BC.

a   b

Plate XXI: *a*. Canopic urn, the cover, which probably does not belong, in the form of a man's head, from Todi, H. of head 0.285, of urn 0.37 [1892.31]. *b*. Pottery throne with bosses, imitating bronze, from Sarteano, H. 0.395 (Pr.361), 6th century BC.

TERRACOTTAS

The sixth and early fifth centuries were a time of monumental building in Etruria and Latium, and the temples built in the sanctuaries must have been impressive buildings. Vitruvius, writing in the time of Augustus, lays down requisites for the arrangement of an Etruscan temple. It should be almost square with a front porch supported by four columns. The interior should be divided into three rooms (*cellae*), there should be no opening in the back. Excavation of Temple A at Pyrgi has shown that this type of temple was established by the early 5th century BC. Marble was not quarried in any quantity before the Roman period and, although the Etruscan temple was built on stone foundations, the superstructure was of wood. These wooden parts were protected from the weather and at the same time decorated by brightly coloured baked clay, mould-made plaques and tiles (architectural terracottas). Large terracotta statues decorated the temple roof. The Museum has recently been given a great number of architectural terracotta fragments of quite outstanding quality. From these it has been possible to reconstruct four separate scenes: chariot racing, pairs of riders (Pl. XXII), processions moving to left and right. There are also lion-head water spouts. Terracottas from the same series have been found at Cisterna di Latina south of Rome and at Sant'-Omobono in Rome itself. The East Greek influence on these is immediately

55

Plate XXII: Terracotta terminal tile; pairs of riders, beneath the horses a hare, hound and deer, given by Mr N. Koutoulakis, L. 0.70. Second half of the 6th century BC.

apparent, but again, as in the case of Pontic vases (p.   ), the artists have selected motifs from other sources. It is not clear in what way these influences were absorbed, whether directly through Ionians or others from overseas, or indirectly through imports. What is clear is that these terracotta plaque makers, working from a long tradition of architectural terracotta manufacture going back to the seventh century BC, were considerably influenced by East Greek art or artists about 530 BC. The style developed on Italian soil and a highly successful amalgam was achieved which suited Etruscan and Latin tastes. It is not known where the Ashmolean terracottas were made. Veii was one important centre for such material but there were many others.

New excavations at Murlo near Siena have turned up hundreds of terracottas which decorated the various buildings of this political and religious centre. At Acquarossa architectural terracottas were used to decorate houses from the late seventh century.

STONEWORK

Although remarkable results were achieved in baked clay, in Etruria, unlike Greece, the lack of any good hard stone curtailed large-scale statuary. The best materials available were the various kinds of volcanic stone (*tufa* and *nenfro*), and soft limestone found only inland. Some stone sculpture, however, was attempted and a characteristic feature at Vulci was the use of large stone creatures as guardians at the entrance to the tombs (Pl. XXIIIa). The inland town of Chiusi also acquired a reputation for stone carving. *Cippi* (four-sided or round pedestals marking a tomb) cut from soft

b

a

Plate XXIII: *a.* Stone lion, part of the wings missing, H. 0.905 [1963.32], sixth century BC. *b.* Part of a limestone funerary *cippus*, Top 0.29 × 0.29 [1933.1646], early 5th century BC.

limestone were carved in low relief with figures of dancers (Pl. XXIIIb), mourners and banqueters. The style of the *cippi* made at the end of the sixth century can be related to the Caeretan *hydriai* and tomb paintings.

SEALS

Etruscan artists and craftsmen excelled in jewellery making and in the manufacture of seals. Seals had been used from an early date (Fig. 6). Around the middle of the sixth century Greek cornelian scarabs began to arrive in Etruria and it is probable that Greek immigrant craftsmen were setting up workshops. These artists inspired a style which can be called Etruscan, the earliest worker in which was the so-called Master of the Boston Dionysos (Pl. XVIIIb). The favourite material of the Etruscan workshops was cornelian. The shape of the seal was invariably a scarab, the beetle worked with great attention to detail. Several Etruscan scarabs are decorated with mythological scenes and some are inscribed (Pl. XVIIIc-d). In the fifth century a style began which depended on the drill for its decorative effect and which developed in the fourth century as the *a globolo* style (Pl. XVIIIe). Seals of this type have been found all over Italy and it is not certain where they were made.

METALWORKING

The skill of Etruscan bronzesmiths, based on a long tradition of metal-working in the area and the ready availability of ores, was well known in the ancient world. Etruscan bronzes travelled a long way, to northern Europe and to the mainland of Greece. The bronze industry—its scale deserves this title—flourished in a number of regional workshops, each of which developed its own style, and reached its height in the later Archaic period (*c.* 540-470 BC). Vulci is thought to have been one of the most important centres of metalworking; certainly the graves at Vulci have produced a great number of bronze objects. The style shows Ionian influence at first, and Attic later. Although influenced by Greek art 'the Etruscan artist shows a definite independence in his attitude towards it. He was certainly skilful enough to produce an exact copy of a Greek model but he had a taste of his own. This is clearly reflected in work of the later fifth and the fourth century BC when he preferred archaic formulae to Classical realism, although he was well aware of the trends in Greece.

The Etruscans specialised in making bronze tripods (Pl. XXIVb) and decorative candlesticks (candelabra). The prongs for the candles were set on top of a tall column often surmounted by a little statuette, which was sometimes of the highest quality (Pl. XXV). The range of goods made in Etruria was enormous; arms and armour, horse trappings and chariot and furniture fittings, small dress articles such as safety pins and belts, everyday

Plate XXIV: *a*. Bronze Etruscan lion, perhaps from a mobile hearth, H. 0.13 [1948.195], 6th century BC. *b*. Fitting from the apex of the outer strut of an Etruscan bronze tripod of the Ornate Group. Formerly Spencer-Churchill Collection, H. 0.136 [1965.290], 5th century BC.

59

Plate XXV: The upper part of an Etruscan bronze candelabrum, a woman and little boy surmount the prongs onto which candles fitted, from near Lake Trasimene, H. 0.182 (G.404). 5th century BC.

Plate XXVI: Etruscan bronzes. Jug, the lower handle terminal in the form of a siren, on the base an inscription Sterthinas (of Stertinius). Formerly Bomford Collection, H. 0.227 [1971.820]. Small round-mouthed jug, the lower handle terminal in the form of a lion, H. 0.17 [1961.364]. Jug the upper handle terminals in the form of tiny lions, the lower spirals and palmette, H. 0.293 [1959.372]. Ladle with duck's head terminal, L. 0.33 (Fortnum B.160). 5th century BC.

cooking utensils, elaborately decorated jugs and ladles (Pl. XXVI). Small statuettes were used as embellishments on a variety of objects (Pls. XXIVa, XXVIIa-c); others were dedicated in temples or placed as offerings in the sanctuaries. A very different style developed in northern Etruria. This can be seen in a votive figure which was found during excavations at Fiesole and was probably made in the area (Pl. XXVIII).

One larger votive figure, perhaps made at Vulci, is illustrated on the cover of this guide. It is of particular interest, for it was ploughed up at Uffington in Oxfordshire, although there is no certainty that it reached England in antiquity. It is related to two other large statuettes found at the site of a mountain shrine up the valley of the Reno (Monteguragazza) on the route from Etruria to Bologna (Felsina), which was a flourishing

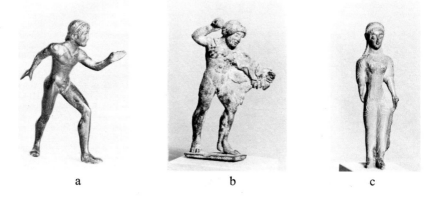

a   b   c

Plate XXVII: Bronze stat-
uettes. *a*. Herakles wearing
lionskin, from a vessel, H. 0.095
[1888.1472]. 5th century BC. *b*.
Athlete, given by Sir John
Beazley, H. 0.083 [1966.605].
Late 6th century BC. *c*. Pair of
winged figures, helmet fittings,
from Palestrina, H. 0.029
(Fortnum B.37, 38). 5th century
BC. *d*. Female votary. Formerly
Spencer-Churchill Collection,
H. 0.096 [1965.289]. Late 6th
century BC.

d

Plate XXVIII: Bronze statuette of a youthful votary, from Fiesole, H. with tangs 0.155 [1977.235]. Early 5th century BC.

63

Etruscan town. They date from the second quarter of the fifth century BC. The Ashmolean figure is dressed in an early example of the toga, and wears pointed shoes with wings, which identify it as Turms (the Etruscan Hermes).

Etruria, although the most famous, was by no means the only area producing fine bronzes. Campania, particularly in the sixth and fifth centuries, was another centre for bronze workshops. Especially successful were those making large cauldrons decorated with statuettes in the round. The little figure of a man carrying a ram (Pl. XXIXa) may have ornamented

a   b

Plate XXIX: *a*. Campanian bronze figure of a man carrying a sheep, from S. Maria di Capua, H. 0.12 (Fortnum B.89). Early 5th century BC. *b*. Bronze figure from a kottabos stand, H. 0.099 (G.433). 4th century BC.

the lid of one such vessel. Etruria's neighbour to the east, Umbria, was by the end of the sixth century producing her own votive bronzes, which were strongly influenced by the earlier geometric style. Fine warriors of the fifth century from Umbria (Pl. XXX), contrast with the more ordinary votive bronzes, little figures placed in the sanctuaries, which were far less carefully made. Bronzework was also carried out in Picenum, and from the Archaic Period became more and more fussy; belts and buckets with

Plate XXX: Bronze warriors, both said to be from Umbria, H. 0.28; 0.265, without tangs (Fortnum B.6, B.7). 5th century BC.

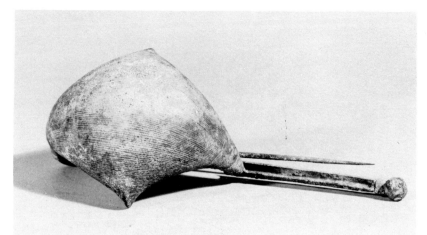

Plate XXXI: Large bronze brooch, the foot terminating in a human head, L. 0.27 (Pr.283). 7th-6th century BC.

swing handles were decorated with fantastic animals; sometimes the fibulae were of vast size, the catchplate decorated with a human or animal head (Pl. XXXI).

The style found in northern Italy, in the Po valley and to the north and east, on bronze objects from about 600 BC has been given the name 'situla art', after bronze buckets (*situlae*). The buckets were decorated with figured scenes reflecting strong north Etruscan influence. A bronze bucket in the Ashmolean illustrates one branch of this art: found in a grave at Vace, Yugoslavia, it is decorated with a frieze of goats accompanied by a man wearing a cloak and flat cap.

VIII The Later Classical and Hellenistic Periods

The later fifth century was a time of withdrawal by the Etruscans from their far-flung territories. Etruscan power in Latium had been broken and the overland routes to Campania were cut. In 423 BC Capua, the most important city in Campania, was captured by the tribes from the barren hilly inland region of Samnium. This was a poor area with few minerals, but the inhabitants, as recent excavations have shown, were by no means backward. The Samnites occupied Cumae three years later and were to become involved with Rome in a series of bitter wars over the control of Campania. The Samnites were noted for their aggression and had charac-

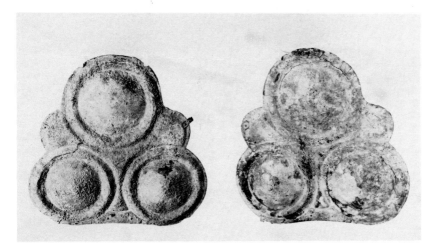

a

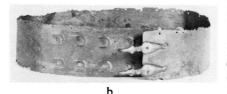

b

Plate XXXII: Bronze breast and backplate. On loan from the National Museum of Wales, Cardiff, Lord Howard de Walden Collection, H. 0.286; bronze belt. Given by Mr A. Castellani, L. 0.244 [1871.99]. Samnite 4th century BC.

67

Plate XXXIII: 'The Flight of the Vestal Virgins', by 'Utili' working 1476-1504 AD. Fox-Strangways Gift.

teristic military equipment, which included a leather-backed bronze belt with elaborate fasteners and a trefoil disc cuirass to protect the chest and back (Pl. XXXII).

After 474 BC, when the Etruscans were defeated at the sea battle off Cumae by the forces of Hieron of Syracuse, the Tyrrhenian coast was vunerable to attack by Syracusan raiders. The raids culminated in the sack of Pyrgi, the rich port of Cerveteri, in 384 BC.

In the north a new threat appeared from Celtic tribesmen, who had crossed the Alps in the fifth century BC. They swept south, were repulsed by the Etruscans but were more successful against Rome and in 390 BC the city was burnt after the battle of Allia. The sack of Rome and the 'Flight of the Vestal Virgins' to Cerveteri is the subject of a fifteenth-century painting in the Museum (Pl. XXXIII). The Celts also overran part of Picenum, and there is ample archaeological evidence to show that they were firmly entrenched in the Po valley by the mid fourth century BC.

Rome was the greatest threat to Etruscan supremacy, and by 396 BC she had taken the neighbouring Etruscan city of Veii. The systematic reduction of the Etruscan cities and the planting of Roman colonies in Etruscan territory continued throughout the fourth and third centuries until the independence of the Etruscan city states was at an end.

Etruscan art, although under considerable political pressures, continued to flourish in many fields in the fourth century. There was something of a revival after a rather stagnant period in the second half of the fifth century. Even in the third century, when Etruria was politically integrated into the Roman federation, there is nothing specifically 'Roman' in Etruscan art. Indeed it is quite clear that until the second century at least, Rome was still largely dependent on Etruscan craftsmen.

POTTERY

The Etruscans still continued to be producers of fine pottery. The earliest red figure vase in the collection is a stamnos (Pl. XXXIV). The handles are in the form of sea monsters. On the one side Zeus and Ganymede are portrayed, on the other a Gigantomachy. Athena struggles with a giant, a scene that is very common in Greek art. Etruscan artists often used Attic vases as models which they faithfully copied. The scene on our stamnos may be Greek but there are many Etruscan features: note for example, the expressive face of Athena and the swooping bird.

During the fourth century the output of red figure vases was prolific. New schools developed and one important centre of manufacture was not in Etruria but in the neighbouring Faliscan territory. Faliscan vases were influenced by Attic vase painters and by South Italian wares made in the Greek colonies. The precise location of some Etruscan potteries is unknown, Cerveteri and Tarquinia were certainly production centres, and probably Vulci and Chiusi. Decorative vases in the shape of a duck

Plate XXXIV: Etruscan red-figure stamnos, by the Painter of the Oxford
Ganymede, the handles in the form of intertwined seamonsters. Side B. Athena
and a Giant, Hermes looks on. Given by Mr E. P. Warren, H. 0.37 [1917.54].
First half of the 4th century BC.

a

b

Plate XXXV: *a*. Red figure duck askos, the body decorated with a flying winged woman (Lasa) carrying armour. The Clusium Group. Given by Miss O. Rhys, L. 0.29 [1951.390]. 4th century BC. *b*. Red figure plate, Genucilia Group, by the Louvre Painter, D. 0.153 [1925.618]. Late 4th century BC.

71

Plate XXXVI: Black glaze jug, the Malacena Group. Given by Mr E. P. Warren, H. to rim 0.232 [1928.50]. 4th-3rd century BC.

(Pl. XXXVa), may have been made at Chiusi. Often the body was decorated with a flying winged female divinity (*lasa*), or a woman's head. Small plates decorated with a woman's head or a star (Pl. XXXVb) were particularly popular in the last decades of the fourth century. This type is known as the Genucilia Group, named from an inscribed plate in Providence, Rhode Island. These plates are thought to have been made in Cerveteri and Falerii.

Etruscan potteries also, in common with those of Latium and Campania, made plain black vases. Often these were close copies of metal vessels, even imitating the handles. Manufacture continued through the third century. Some of the finest examples belong to the Malacena class named after the site near Monteriggioni (Pl. XXXVI).

In Apulia, besides the red figure vases made in the Greek colonies, painted vases of three distinct but related types were being made in the 'native potteries'. Regional styles, Daunian (in the north), Peucetian (in the centre) and Messapian (in the south), had evolved in the eighth century BC and continued into the fourth and third centuries. The Daunian vases illustrated (Fig. 16a, b) come from potteries situated round Ruvo and Canosa. By the third quarter of the fourth century, the type of decoration and the traditional shape disintegrated under Greek influence. During the last quarter of the century the use of the fast wheel in pottery-making further transformed styles and a distinctive Late Canosan ware was being made (Fig. 16c). Messapian vases are nearly all of typical shape with high handles decorated with disks (Fig. 16d).

All the vases we have seen were part of best 'dinner services'. Most come from tombs and the early excavators discarded plainer wares as rubbish. Everyday pottery and kitchen ware seldom found their way into museum collections.

METALWORKING

During the fourth century and later the bronze industry still produced fine pieces. The most notable is the big bronze chimaera found at Arezzo in 1553, now in Florence, which was restored by no less an artist than Benvenuto Cellini. Many more mundane statuettes and vessels were produced (Pl. XXXVII), and new types were introduced alongside the traditional articles. The game of *kottabos* became popular and kottabos stands have been found in a number of graves. The game supplied an after-dinner diversion on convivial occasions. Invented perhaps by the Greek colonists in Sicily it was adopted by the Etruscans and Latins. The player, from his couch, would aim the dregs in his wine cup at a metal disc placed on top of the stand. If his aim was true the disc fell onto a second disc set lower down the shaft. Small figures sometimes formed part of the stand (Pl. XXIXb). This statuette is appropriately of a player aiming his cup.

73

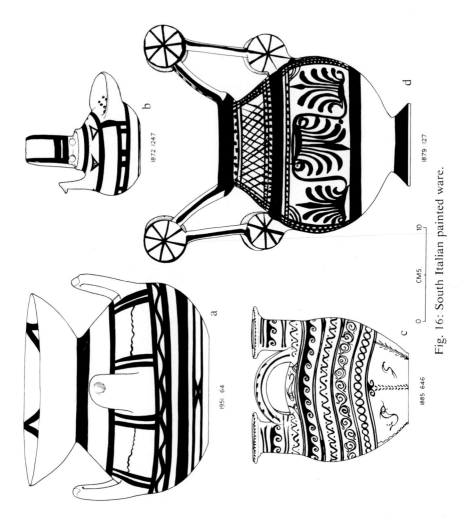

Fig. 16: South Italian painted ware.

74

Plate XXXVII: Bronzes. Jug, Sant'Anatolia type, H. 0.095 [1932.193]. Vase in the shape of a woman's head, H. 0.145 (Fortnum B.287). Acrobat, the handle of a cista, from Palestrina, L. 0.077 [1888.1474]. 4th century BC.

Bronze mirrors, which had been made from about 500 BC came increasingly into favour in the fourth century (Pl. XXXVIII). The front was highly polished, the back was engraved or had figures in relief. Often the figures are identified by inscriptions, gods and goddesses and various Greek mythological scenes. Other examples of Greek mythological scenes are found on cinerary urns made of alabaster at Volterra (Pl. XXXIX), and of clay at Chiusi (Pl. XL), mainly in the third and second centuries BC. The fragmentary alabaster urn (Pl. XXXIX) shows Odysseus and the sirens: the sirens sit on rocks playing musical instruments while Odysseus is restrained by his companions. On the clay urn (Pl. XL) the tragic fight between the Theban brothers Polynices and Eteocles is enacted. Many of the Etruscan gods were taken from the Greek pantheon (cover), but there is no reason to believe that the Etruscans accepted Greek religion. The Etruscan belief was in a revealed religion and much emphasis was placed on the art of divination. We know that much of the doctrine was written in books, although these are now lost to us. These books dealt with specific areas of religion. The *Libri Rituales* gave the rules for founding cities and

Plate XXXVIII: Bronze mirror, engraved on the back the Judgment of Paris.
Formerly Ravizza Collection, given by Mr A. Castellani D. 0.17 [1871.97]. 4th
century BC.

Plate XXXIX: The front of an alabaster cinerary urn. Odysseus and the sirens some reworking L. 0.63 (Oldfield 64). 2nd century BC.

Plate XL: Terracotta cinerary urn. Winged figures watch the combat between Polynices and Eteocles, L. 0.43 [1885.568]. 2nd century BC.

building temples; other books described the art of *haruspices*, the reading by the priests of the entrails of sacrificed animals.

TERRACOTTAS

Terracotta offerings (Pl. XLI) found in votive deposits in the Latin and Etruscan sanctuaries seem to show that there was a strong connection between religion and medicine. The offerings varied from sanctuary to sanctuary, and it has been suggested that different sanctuaries may have specialised in curing different diseases. The excavation of the sanctuary at Ponte di Nona near Rome, undertaken by Dr T. Potter on behalf of the British School at Rome and Lancaster University, discovered over 8,000 terracotta offerings, mostly heads, feet, hands and limbs. Other sanctuaries have yielded a preponderance of sexual organs and other anatomical models.

Plate XLI: Votive terracottas, heads, foot, womb and hand, H. of larger head 0.255 [1885.675-6; 1909.349i, e, from Veii, given by Mr T. Ashby; 1872.1308]. 3rd-2nd century BC.

The votive terracottas are, on the whole, crude mass-produced works. The tradition of fine terracotta making, however, still existed and many statues for decorating temples were made in the fourth and third centuries. A magnificent team of winged horses from a chariot group at Tarquinia, is an example of Etruscan art, rivalling any Greek creation in this material. A very fine head, over life-size (Pl. XLII), was found at Rome on the Esquiline. The strongly hellenising style has led many scholars to consider that it was made by a Greek craftsman working in Rome about 300 BC. Others see it as yet another example of the art of an Etruscan under strong Greek influence. Speculation about the birthplace of such an artist is perhaps meaningless.

By the end of the second century Rome had become mistress of the Hellenistic world. Works of art in their hundreds were removed to Rome from Syracuse, Asia Minor, Corinth and elsewhere, looted after each successful campaign. The presence of genuine Greek works of art, statues, paintings and vases, can hardly have failed to play a large part in the hellenising of Etruscan art. Rome was now becoming the greatest patron of art not only in Italy but in the whole ancient world, and was virtually independent of Etruscan artists for the first time.

Plate XLII: Terracotta head of a youth, found on the Esquiline Hill at Rome, H. 0.294. (Fortnum S.1). *c.* 300 BC.

IX Ancient Italy: Bibliography (by D. Ridgway)

A fully representative list with the above title would be at least as long again as this guide. I have therefore tried to combine a bare minimum of general works (which usually have their own extensive bibliographies) with at least some items of more specific relevance to the topics covered in the preceding text—where choices have naturally been determined by the nature of the pre-Roman Italian collection in the Museum. Throughout, I have been guided by a preference for recent (i.e. post 1970) works, if possible in English. The following abbreviations have been used for three new and frequently cited collective volumes:-

IBR Ridgway, D. and F. R., eds., *Italy before the Romans: the Iron Age, Orientalizing and Etruscan periods* (London and New York: Academic Press, 1979).

PCIA Popoli e Civiltà dell'Italia Antica. Rome: Biblioteca di Storia Patria, 1974-1978 (seven volumes).

PIA Blake, H. McK., Potter, T. W., Whitehouse, D. B., eds. *Papers in Italian Archaeology, I* (British Archaeological Reports Supplementary Series, 41: in two parts). Oxford, 1978.

I. PREHISTORIC ITALY

General items (see also Section IV, below):

Barfield, L. *Northern Italy before Rome* (London: Thames and Hudson, 1971)

Barker, G. 'The conditions of cultural and economic growth in the Bronze Age of central Italy', in *Proc. Prehist. Soc.*, xxxviii (1972), pp. 170-208.

'Prehistoric territories and economies in central Italy', in Higgs, E. S., ed., *Palaeoeconomy* (Cambridge: University Press, 1974), pp. 111-175.

Bernabò Brea, L. *Sicily before the Greeks*, 2nd ed. (London: Thames and Hudson, 1966)

Graziosi, P. *L'arte preistorica in Italia* (Florence: Sansoni, 1973)

Peroni, R. *Archeologia della Puglia preistorica* (Rome: De Luca, 1967)

Radmilli, A. M., ed. *Guida della preistoria italiana* (Florence: Sansoni, 1975)

Trump, D. H. *Central and Southern Italy before Rome* (London: Thames and Hudson, 1966)

Whitehouse, R. 'Italian prehistory, carbon 14 and the tree-ring calibration', *PIA*, pp. 71-91.

Areas and topics, Neolithic to Early Bronze Age:

Bagolini, B. & Biagi, P. 'Current culture history issues in the study of the Neolithic of Northern Italy', in *Univ. London, Inst. of Archaeology Bulletin*, xiv (1977), pp.143-166.

81

Hallam, B. R. *et alii* 'Obsidian in the Western Mediterranean', in *Proc. Prehist. Soc.*, xlii (1976), pp. 85-110.

Peroni, R. *L'età del bronzo nella penisola italiana, I: l'antica età del bronzo* (Florence: Olschki 1971)

Whitehouse, R. 'The last hunter-gatherers in southern Italy', in *World Archaeology* ii (1970-1971), pp.239-54

'The Neolithic pottery sequence in southern Italy', in *Proc. Prehist. Soc.*, xxxv (1969), pp. 267-310.

Whitehouse, R. & Renfrew, C. 'The Copper Age of peninsular Italy and the Aegean', in *Annual of the British School at Athens* lxix (1974), pp. 343-390.

The definitive report on the Society of Antiquaries Tavoliere research project is still awaited; see meanwhile Bradford, J., *Ancient Landscapes: studies in field archaeology* (London: Bell, 1957), pp. 85-110; and most recently Whitehouse, R., in *Proc. Prehist. Soc.* xl (1974), p. 203f. Recent Italian excavations at Passo di Corvo: Tiné, S., in *Antike Welt* 3 (1975), pp. 27-32.

Areas and topics, Middle to Final Bronze Age; and Mycenaeans:

Bietti Sestieri, A. M. 'The metal industry of continental Italy, 13th-11th century, and its Aegean connections', in *Proc. Prehist. Soc.*, xxxix (1973), pp.383-424.

Fugazzola Delpino, M. A. *Testimonianze di cultura appenninica nel Lazio* (Florence: Sansoni, 1976)

'The Proto-Villanovan: a survey', *IBR* Chapter 2.

Macnamara, E. 'A group of bronzes from Surbo: new evidence for Aegean contacts with Apulia during Mycenaean IIIB and C', in *Proc. Prehist. Soc.*, xxxvi (1970), pp. 241-260.

Marazzi, M. *Egeo e Occidente alla fine del II millennio a.C.* (Rome: Edizioni dell'Ateneo, 1976).

Taylour, *Lord* W. *Mycenaean pottery in Italy and adjacent areas* (Cambridge: University Press, 1958)

Vagnetti, L. 'I Micenei in Italia: la documentazione archeologica', in *Parola del Passato* xxv (1970), pp. 359-380.

II. IRON AGE, ORIENTALIZING AND COLONISTS

There has been no book in any language entitled simply '*The Iron Age in Italy*' since D. Randall-MacIver's of 1927 (Oxford)—which is now more than half-a-century out of date. On the complex issues raised by the above three topics, considered singly or in combination, see:

Buchner, G. 'Early Orientalizing: aspects of the Euboean connection', *IBR* Chapter 5.

Boardman, J. *The Greeks overseas*, 3rd ed. (Thames and Hudson, forthcoming)

Close-Brooks, J. & Ridgway, D. 'Veii in the Iron Age', *IBR* Chapter 4

Colonna, G. 'Preistoria e protostoria di Roma e del Lazio', *PCIA* II, pp.273-346.

de La Genière, J. 'The Iron Age in Southern Italy', *IBR* Chapter 3.

Hencken, H. *Tarquinia, Villanovans and early Etruscans* (Cambridge, Mass., 1968)

Lollini, D. G. 'La civiltà picena', *PCIA* V, pp. 107-195

Potter, T. W. *A Faliscan town in South Etruria: excavations at Narce 1966-1971* (London: British School at Rome, 1976)

Rathje, A. 'Oriental imports in Etruria in the 8th and 7th centuries BC: their origins and implications', *IBR* Chapter 6.

Ridgway, D. 'The first Western Greeks: Campanian coasts and Southern Etruria', in *Greeks, Celts and Romans*, eds. Hawkes, C. and S. (London: Dent, 1973), pp.5-38.

'Early Rome and Latium: an archaeological introduction', *IBR* Chapter 7

Ridgway, F. R. 'The Este and Golasecca cultures: a chronological guide', *IBR* Chapter 15.

Rittatore Vonwiller, F. 'La civiltà del ferro in Lombardia, Piemonte e Liguria', *PCIA* IV, pp. 223-356.

Strøm, I. *Problems concerning the origin and early development of the Etruscan Orientalizing style* (Odense: University Press, 1971)

Zuffa, M. 'La civiltà villanoviana', *PCIA* V, pp. 197-363.

Exhibition catalogue *Civiltà del Lazio primitivo* (Rome, 1976)

III. THE ETRUSCANS AND THEIR NEIGHBOURS

The bibliography, even of items written in or translated into English, is vast. The best book that has ever been written about Etruria is the second (definitive) edition of George Dennis, *Cities and Cemeteries of Etruria* (London, 1878; reprinted 1883; the Everyman's Library reprinted the smaller 1848 edition in 1907). For a more recent British approach to the topography of Etruria, see the South Etruria survey articles and volumes in the *Papers of the British School at Rome*, 1955 onwards; and Potter, T. W., *The changing landscape of South Etruria* (London: Elek, 1979) and general accounts of the Etruscans themselves:-

Banti, L. *Etruscan cities and their culture* (London: Batsford, 1973)

Cristofani, M. *The Etruscans: a new investigation* (London: Orbis, 1979)

Heurgon, J. *Daily life of the Etruscans* (London: Weidenfeld and Nicolson, 1964)

The rise of Rome to 264 BC (London: Batsford, 1973)

Macnamara, E. *Everyday life of the Etruscans* (London: Batsford, 1973)

Pallottino, M. *The Etruscans*, 2nd English edition (London: Allen Lane, 1975; Harmondsworth: Pelican, 1978)

Richardson, E. *The Etruscans: their art and civilization*, 2nd ed. (Chicago: University Press, 1976)

Scullard, H. H. *The Etruscan cities and Rome* (London: Thames and Hudson, 1967)

Of the above, Pallottino's Pelican is probably still the best basic text-book; Macnamara's is a simpler book which assembles much basic information; and Cristofani's incorporates the results of several profitable new approaches to Etruscan material. The standard illustrated corpus of Etruscan art by G. Q. Giglioli, *L'Arte Etrusca* (Milan, 1935), has now been replaced by Sprenger, M. and Bartoloni, G., *Die Etrusker: Kunst und Geschichte* (Munich: Hirmer, 1977); and Etruscan places are beautifully illustrated (and accompanied by a reliable and up-to-date text) in Boitani, F., Cataldi, M., Pasquinucci, M., *Etruscan cities* (London: Cassell, 1975). Treatments, mainly recent, of individual aspects of Etruscan art and civilization (and of those of their contemporaries in Italy) include the following:-

Andrén, A. *Osservazioni sulle terrecotte architettoniche etrusco-italiche* (Stockholm: *Lectiones Boëthianae* i, 1971)

Beazley, J. D. *Etruscan vase-painting* (Oxford: Clarendon Press, 1947)
'The world of the Etruscan mirror' in *J. Hellenic Studies*, lxix (1949), pp. 1-17.

Boëthius, A. & Ward-Perkins, J. B. *Etruscan and Roman architecture* (Harmondsworth: Penguin History of Art, 1970)

Bonfante, L. 'The women of Etruria', in *Arethusa* vi (1973), pp. 91-101; and see also *Archaeology* xxvi (1973), pp. 242-249.
Etruscan dress (Baltimore and London: Johns Hopkins University Press, 1975)
'Etruscan influence in Northern Italy', in *Archaeological News* (Tallahassee), v (1976), pp. 93-106.

Brendel, O. J. *Etruscan Art* (Harmondsworth: Penguin History of Art, 1979)

Brown, A. C. 'Etrusco-Italic architectural terra-cottas in the Ashmolean Museum, Oxford', in *Archaeological Reports for 1973-74*, pp. 60-65.

Brown, W. Ll. *The Etruscan lion* (Oxford: Clarendon Press, 1960)

Colonna, G. *Bronzi votivi umbro-sabellici a figura umana, I: periodo 'arcaico'* (Florence: Sansoni, 1970)
'Basi conoscitive per una storia economica dell'Etruria', in *Supplemento Annali 22, Istituto Italiano di Numismatica* (1975), pp. 3-23.
'The later Orientalizing period in Rome', *IBR* Chapter 9

Cornell, T. J. 'Etruscan historiography', in *Annali della Scuola Normale Superiore di Pisa*³ vi (1976), pp. 411-439.
'The foundation of Rome in the ancient literary tradition', *PIA*, pp.131-139.

Cristofani, M. 'Il "dono" nell'Etruria arcaica', in *Parola del Passato*, xxx (1975), pp. 132-152.
'Recent advances in Etruscan epigraphy and language', *IBR* Chapter 14.

D'Agostino, B. 'Il mondo periferico della Magna Grecia', *PCIA* II, pp. 177-271.

Del Chiaro, M. A. *Etruscan Red-figured Vase painting at Caere* (Berkeley and London: University of California Press, 1975)

Frederiksen, M. W. 'The Etruscans in Campania' *IBR* Chapter 11.

Gantz, T. N. 'The Tarquin dynasty', in *Historia* xxiv (1975), pp. 539-554.

Gras, M. 'La piraterie tyrrhénienne en Mer Égée: mythe ou realité?' in *L'Italie préromaine et la Rome républicaine: Mélanges Heurgon* (Rome: École Française, 1976), pp. 341-370.

Hannestad, L. 'The Paris Painter' and 'The followers of the Paris Painter', in *Det Kongelige Danske Videnskabernes Selskab Historkisk-filosofiske Meddelelser* 47, 2 (1974), and 47, 4 (1976).

Harris, W. V. *Rome in Etruria and Umbria* (Oxford: Clarendon Press, 1971)

Hemelrijk, J. M. *De Caeretaanse Hydriae* (Rotterdam, 1956) and *Caeretan Hydriae* (Mainz, forthcoming)

Jehasse, J. and L. 'The Etruscans and Corsica', *IBR* Chapter 12.

Johansen, F. *Reliefs en bronze d'Étrurie* (Copenhagen: Ny Carlsberg Glyptothek, 1971)

Mansuelli, G. A. 'Le sens architectural dans les peintures des tombes tarquiniennes avant l'époque hellénistique', in *Revue Archéologique* i (1976), pp. 41-74.

'The Etruscan city', *IBR* Chapter 13.

Pallottino, M. *Etruscan painting* (Geneva: Skira, 1952); and, for colour pictures of more tombs, Moretti, M.: *Nuovi monumenti della pittura etrusca a Tarquinia* (Milan: Lerici, 1966)

Civiltà artistica etrusco-italica (Florence: Sansoni, 1971)

Rasmussen, T. *Bucchero Pottery from Southern Etruria* (Cambridge, 1979)

Riccioni, G. 'Vulci: a topographical and cultural survey', *IBR* Chapter 10.

Salmon, E. T. *Samnium and the Samnites* (Cambridge: University Press, 1967)

Stibbe, C. M. 'Pontic vases in Oxford', *in Mededelingen van het Nederlands Instituut te Rome*, xxxix (1977), pp. 7-12.

Szilágyi, J. G. *Etruszko-korinthosi vázafestészet* (Budapest: Apollo könyvtár vi, 1975)

Torelli, M. 'Tre studi di storia etrusca', in *Dialoghi di Archeologia* viii (1974-1975), pp. 3-78.

There is much more in the *Forma Italiae, Studi e materiali di Etruscologia e Antichità Italiche, Monumenti Etruschi* and other Italian monograph series. New discoveries in Central Italy and Magna Grecia are summarized at regular intervals in *Archaeological Reports* (London: Hellenic Society with British School at Athens); new Italian and other relevant books may be reviewed in the *American Journal of Archaeology* and in the *Journal of Roman Studies*. Attic vases in and from Italy are listed in the late Sir John Beazley's *Attic Black-figure Vase-painters, Attic Red-figure Vase-painters*[2] and *Paralipomena* (Oxford: 1956, 1963, 1971) and, by museums, in the fascicules of the *Corpus Vasorum Antiquorum*; they are also discussed by J. Boardman, *Athenian Black Figure Vases* and *Athenian Red Figure Vases: the Archaic Period* (London: Thames and Hudson 1974, 1975). For South Italian vases, see A.D. Trendall, *The Red-figured Vases of Lucania, Campania and Sicily* (Oxford, 1967, with *Supplements* 1970 and 1973; A.D. Trendall, *South Italian vase painting* (The British Museum, 1966); A.D. Trendall and A. Cambitoglou, *The Red-figured vases of Apulia*, Vol. I (Oxford, 1978).

IV. ITALY AND EUROPE

Italy is obviously a 'classical land': but throughout the period reviewed in this guide her archaeology is intimately bound up with that of Central and Western Europe, too. General accounts of Italy's European context will be found in:-

Harding, D. W. *Prehistoric Europe* (Oxford: Elsevier-Phaidon, 1978)
Piggott, S. *Ancient Europe* (Edinburgh: University Press, 1965)
Sandars, N. K. *Prehistoric Art in Europe* (Harmondsworth: Penguin History of Art, 1968)

Particular periods, from the Neolithic to the Celtic Iron Age, are treated in:-

Phillips, P. *Early farmers of West Mediterranean Europe* (London: Hutchinson, 1975)
Daniel, G. E. *The megalith builders of Western Europe* (Harmondsworth: Pelican, 1963)
Mercer, R., ed. *Beakers in Britain and Europe* (British Archaeological Reports Supplementary Series, 26). Oxford 1977.
Coles, J. M. and Harding, A. F. *The Bronze Age in Europe* (London: Methuen, 1979)
Müller-Karpe, H. *Beiträge zur Chronologie der Urnenfelderzeit nördlich und südlich der Alpen* (Berlin: De Gruyter, 1959)
von Merhart, G. *Hallstatt und Italien: Gesammelte Aufsätze zur frühen Eisenzeit in Italien und Mitteleuropa* (collected papers, ed. Kossack, G.) (Mainz, 1969)
Megaw, J. V. S. *Art of the European Iron Age* (Bath: Adams and Dart, 1970)
Dehn, W. & Frey, O. H. 'Southern imports and the Hallstatt and Early La Tène chronology of Central Europe', *IBR* Chapter 16
Hawkes, C. F. C. 'Runes and the caput Adriae', in *Adriatica* (*Miscellanea G. Novak*; Zagreb, 1970), pp. 399-408.
Exhibition catalogue *I Galli e l'Italia* (Rome, 1978)

In addition, much Italian material has been published in the two principal European series of *corpora*: *Inventaria Archaeologica* (by site: Bronze Age hoards) and *Prähistorische Bronzefunde* (by type: horse-bits, swords, pins, wheeled vehicles, knives so far; fibulas in preparation).

On Etruria and 19th century British taste and travel, see G. Colonna, 'Archeologia dell'età romantica in Etruria', in *Studi Etruschi* 46, 1978, pp. 81-117 (with a full account of the Campanari exhibition of 1837 in Pall Mall); and D. E. Rhodes, *Dennis of Etruria* (London: C. and A. Woolf, 1973). On the 18th century, see B. Fothergill, *Sir William Hamilton: Envoy Extraordinary* (London: Faber and Faber, 1969); and E. Clay and M. Frederiksen, *Sir William Gell in Italy* (London: H. Hamilton, 1976).